The Public and the Police

The Public and the Police

An Extended Summary of the Aims,
Methods and Findings
of a Three-Part Enquiry
into the Relations Between the
London Public and its Metropolitan
Police Force

Proposed and directed by
William A. Belson B.A., Ph.D.
as Head of the Survey Research Centre
of the London School of Economics
and Political Science

Harper & Row, Publishers
London, New York, Evanston, San Francisco

Published by Harper & Row
28 Tavistock Street, London WC2E 7PN

Standard Book Number 06-318025-1

Designed by Millions
Typeset by Preface Ltd, Salisbury, Wiltshire
Printed by Biddles Ltd, Guildford, Surrey

Contents

The Three Parts of the Inquiry

This extended summary is based upon the findings of three closely related enquiries

I
A study of the attitudes, beliefs and behaviour of adults in London in relation to the Metropolitan Police Force.

II
A study of the attitudes, beliefs and behaviour of young people in London in relation to the Metropolitan Police Force.

III
A study of the attitudes, beliefs and behaviour of police officers in the Metropolitan Force in relation to the London public.

The three enquiries have been reported separately and the reports are held by the Metropolitan Police Force.

Personnel principally engaged in the inquiry

Design and direction
William A. Belson B.A., Ph.D.

Research Team
Lindsay L. Brook, M.A.
Linda L. Light, B.A.
Wendy King, B.Sc.
Gil A. Williams, B.A.

Data Processing
Vernon R. Thompson
Joan Rowat

Materials and Equipment
Jean M. Carr

Introduction and Acknowledgements

INTRODUCTION

This report is an extended summary of the results of three studies of the relationship between the London public and the Metropolitan Police Force which were carried out at the request of the Commissioner of the Metropolis and with the agreement of the Home Office.

All three studies arose from recommendations put forward by Dr W. A. Belson in 1966 in his confidential report to the late Sir Joseph Simpson, 'Public Relations in the Metropolitan Police Force — Recommendations For Research as a Basis for Policy and Action'. Dr Belson was responsible for the design of the inquiries and they have been conducted under his direction.

The three studies were concerned with:

1 The attitudes, beliefs and behaviour of the adult population of London in relation to the Metropolitan Police Force (based on a 1,200-person sample).

2 The attitudes, beliefs and behaviour of 13 to 20-year-old Londoners in relation to the Metropolitan Police Force (based on a 503-person sample).

3 The attitudes, beliefs and behaviour of officers in the Metropolitan Police Force in relation to the London public (based on a 1,000-person sample).

It was intended that between them the three studies would determine the present state of the relationship between the police and the public in London, indicate whether there were grounds for remedial action of any kind and aid the formulation of any such action. Particular emphasis was placed on discovering ways of increasing the amount of help given to the police by the public.

Each study has been the subject of a full report by Dr Belson submitted to the Commissioner, Sir Robert Mark. The present document is an extended summary of all three reports.

ACKNOWLEDGEMENTS

The research personnel most closely involved in this project have been: William A. Belson, D.F.C., B.A., Ph.D., Director of the enquiry and then Head of the Survey Research Centre of the London School of Economics; Lindsay L. Brook, M.A., Linda L. Light, B.A., Wendy King, B.Sc., and Gil A. Williams, B.A. In addition, Joan Rowat was responsible for the editing and coding of questionnaires and Vernon R. Thompson, assisted by Denis Cahalane, was responsible for all aspects of the computer analysis of the data. Jean Carr, Office Manager of the Survey Research Centre, was responsible for the production of all research materials and equipment. The success of the inquiry depended to an important degree upon the skills and the conscientiousness of the interviewers who worked on different phases of the project.

Throughout the project, Dr Belson and members of the research team worked in close liaison with Mr G. D. Gregory, O.B.E., D.S.C., Public Relations Officer of the Metropolitan Police Force, and with Mr J. H. V. Bradley, B.A., Senior Information Officer in the Public Relations Department. Their help and advice is gratefully acknowledged.

A working party consisting of a representative from the Home Office and of senior personnel from New Scotland Yard, was set up expressly to aid the project. Its members provided critical appraisal and suggestions at crucial stages in the inquiry and secured facilities and other forms of aid whenever requested.

The membership of the working party varied during the inquiry and has included, besides Mr Gregory and Mr Bradley, Commander E. L. Williams, Q.P.M. (D5 Branch), Commander F. R. Meyricks (A7 Branch), Commander P. C. Neivens (A7 Branch), Commander V. J. H. Rignell (A7

Branch), the late Commander J. H. Remnant (D5 Branch), Mr R. A. James, M.C. (Home Office), Mr D. H. J. Hilary (Home Office), Mr B. G. David (F Department).

Commander R. Huntley, B.E.M. (C Department) and Chief Superintendent J. Collie (A7 Branch), although not members of the working party, took part in several meetings to advise on areas of special interest.

Whereas Dr Belson and his team take full responsibility for the conduct of the inquiry and for technical decisions throughout it, the help given by the working party and those who assisted it was very considerable and without this help the success of the inquiry would have been very limited.

We wish also to thank the many officers and members of the civilian staff of the Metropolitan Police Force who gave their time and attention to the research team in the period when they were making familiarization visits to the different departments, branches and stations of the Metropolitan Police Force and also those who did so much t assist with the administrative aspects of the survey of police officers.

Thanks are especially due to both the Superintendents' Association and to the Police Federation for their goodwill and their general support.

Finally, the project director, Dr Belson, wishes to make it quite clear that he alone carries the responsibility for the wording of this summary, for the interpretation of the findings reported in it and for the formulation of recommendations.

William A. Belson
Project Director

Aims and the Issues Dealt With

The central aim of the three studies on which this summary is based* was to investigate the attitudinal and the behavioural relationship between the resident population of London and the officers of the Metropolitan Police Force.

The aim of the investigation was to provide information which would contribute, both in its own right and in conjunction with other evidence, to the development of policy and long-term plans directed at maintaining and improving police—public relations in London and, in particular, at remedying any weaknesses which the research may have revealed.

The specific issues detailed for study included not only matters that had at some time been the subject of major public concern, but also matters that serving police officers and ordinary members of the public themselves thought to be important. It was in this context that the three studies between them dealt with a wide range of matters which included the following.

1 The global or generalized reactions of the public to the police (e.g. how satisfied the public is with the police) and the public's views about the characteristics of the police (e.g. in terms of courtesy, calmness, rudeness, honesty). In the *police* survey questions were asked in order to find out to what extent police officers were correct in their views about what the public thought of them.

2 The social philosophy of the police and their views about the characteristics of the public.

*As detailed on p. vii.

3 How the police are perceived by the public as treating certain minorities and population sectors; *police* views about which population sectors produce problems for them and the nature of these problems.

4 The public's views about what the duties of the police should be and about how well the police perform various of their duties; the public's views about how the police behave in certain situations, with special reference to behaviour of a kind likely to affect police—public relations.

5 The views of the police and of the public about the powers of the police.

6 The situations in which the public would contact the police and the attitudes of the public towards helping the police; police views about how helpful the public is.

7 Police views about those aspects of their working conditions and their duties that seem to have a bearing on police—public relations (e.g. wearing a uniform when calling on people at their homes, participation in community affairs, the Home Beat system, the methods used to investigate complaints against the police).

8 The public's knowledge about the duties of policemen and of policing arrangements.

9 Police views about the efficiency of various activities conducted by the police for the betterment of police— public relations; police views about measures that could help to improve police—public relations.

10 The views of police and public about the influence of the different mass media upon police—public relations.

The questions to adults tended to be paralleled by the questions to young people (aged from 12 to 20 years).

Methods Used in the Inquiries

The methods used in the three studies were complex and are described in detail in the three resulting reports. However, because this present document is especially concerned with presenting *findings* and their implications, all that has been done here is to describe certain of the more central aspects of the research methods used.

Preparatory or exploratory work

As background to each study, the research team had taken part in extensive visiting and discussion within selected departments and branches of the Metropolitan Police Force. This was followed by exploratory interviewing of an intensive kind with selected persons: police officers and young people in preparation for the youth survey, police officers and adult members of the public in preparation for the adult survey, and further intensive interviews with police officers in preparation for the police survey. Only in this way could the three surveys be properly geared to the issues and the realities of the scene to be studied.

Questionnaire design

Questionnaire coverage was largely determined by the exploratory meetings and interviews. Their respective coverages and draft forms were subject to discussion with the working party and each questionnaire went through several stages of piloting and modification before being finalized.

The questionnaires were lengthy, were in coloured page sections, and one of their special features was the use of visual aids wherever possible. Each section was introduced

3

with an explanation to the interviewer about its purposes
and each had built into it special instructions and numerous
reminders to interviewers. The questionnaires were mainly
structured in the sense that they offered a choice of
answers, but there were also open-ended questions which
were subject to probing and which were designed to
provide insight into why respondents felt or behaved as
they did.

The survey area and the sampling methods used

For all three surveys, the survey region was the Metropolitan
Police District of London. Within this region multi-stage,
stratified, random sampling was used in each of the three
surveys.

The achieved samples for the three surveys were 1,200
adults, 503 young persons and 1,000 police officers,
representing 81, 97 and 93 per cent respectively of the
target sample members who were eligible and available*.

Interviewing

The interviewers were men and women mainly aged between
the early twenties and the mid-thirties and the majority of
them had a university background. They were selected
after personal interview and underwent extended initial
training. Training was continued throughout the period of
fieldwork. The interviews with adults were conducted
within a survey period of six months, the 'young person'
interviews within a survey period of two months and the
police interviews within a survey period of four months†.
Within a wider system of quality control, all interviews were
tape recorded for critical examination by research staff‡.

---

*By *un*available is meant those members of the public who were too
ill or incapacitated to be interviewed, who spoke no English, who
were away for the duration of the survey period, who had moved
away from the area, who were not at home on each of six calls by
the interviewer. If we include the 'not at homes' and 'did not keep
appointment' in the available sample, the three percentage figures,
representing success levels, become 79, 97 and 90 per cent.
†Members of the public were almost all interviewed at home; with
few exceptions, police officers were interviewed in special
interviewing centres away from their homes and stations.
‡Fieldwork for the investigation was completed in March 1972.

4

Analysis

The analysis of the results was computerized. At this stage the cross-analysis of results was limited to some six or so variables in each survey, but it was agreed that the extensive survey data collected should be readily available for further analysis by or for the police where this seemed to them to be desirable.

Findings

This statement of findings is an integration of the results of all three investigations, presented in the form of an extended summary. As a summary, it is intended to guide the reader quickly to an overall appraisal of the findings, though it inevitably leaves much to be gained from a detailed study of the three basic reports. Within the summary, findings are set out under eleven headings which together encompass the coverage detailed under 'Aims'.

1 SOME GENERALIZED REACTIONS TO AND JUDGMENTS ABOUT THE METROPOLITAN POLICE FORCE

This section of the findings is concerned with several aspects of the public's reactions to the police: their general level of satisfaction with the police, trust of them, liking for them, and so on; how the police interpret the public's reactions to them; how the public rates the police in terms of personal characteristics.

Table 1
How the public reacts to the police and what the police *think* this reaction to be

Level of satisfaction with the police and other global reactions to them

In Table 1 there are presented details of how London adults and young people react to the police and of how the police *think* the public reacts to them.

+ Not offered as a possible answer to the police respondents
— Less than 0.5 per cent
*Based on assumed weights as follows: (i) Most favourable rating = 1, next = 2, next = 3, next = 4, least favourable rating = 5. Hence the lower the mean, the more favourable the rating.
†No usable information

| Reactions to the police | Police impressions of how the public reacts to them | | How the public does in fact react to the police | | | |
| | | | Adults | | Young people | |
	(%)	Mean* rating	(%)	Mean* rating	(%)	Mean* rating
Liking the police						
Like them very much	8	2.19	31	1.81	16	2.16
Quite like them	78		62		69	
Neither like nor dislike them	+		1		1	
Don't like them very much	13		5		13	
Don't like them at all	—		—		2	
No information	1		2		1	
Respect for the police						
A lot of respect	47	1.59	73	1.31	44	1.68
Some respect	48		25		50	
Neither respect nor disrespect	+		0		0	
Not much respect	3		2		5	
No respect at all	0		—		1	
No information†	1		0		—	
Trust of the police						
Trust them completely	11	2.07	30	1.89	25	2.13
Trust them quite a lot	79		60		58	
Neither trust nor distrust them	+		—		—	
Don't trust them very much	9		8		15	
Don't trust them at all	—		1		3	
No information	1		1		—	
Satisfied with the police						
Very satisfied	18	1.88	61	1.48	Not asked	
Fairly satisfied	79		35			
Neither satisfied nor dissatisfied	+		0			
Not very satisfied	3		3			
Not at all satisfied	—		1			
No information	1		—			
Feeling at ease with the police						
Very much at ease	10	2.89	45	1.86	Not asked	
Feeling at ease	41		40			
Neither at ease nor uncomfortable	+		—			
Slightly uncomfortable	46		13			
Very uncomfortable	2		2			
No information	1		2			
Scared of the police						
Not at all scared of them	Not asked		Not asked		45	1.85
Just a bit scared of them					41	
Neither scared nor not scared					0	
Fairly scared of them					12	
Very scared of them					2	
No information					—	

In the *adult sample*, the reaction ratings tended markedly to be favourable. Thus 96 per cent were either fairly or very satisfied with the police, 93 per cent liked them; 98 per cent expressed at least some degree of respect for them including 73 per cent claiming 'a lot of respect' for them; 90 per cent trusted them; 85 per cent felt fairly or completely 'at ease' with them. These generalized ratings do not, in principle, rule out negative reactions at the specific level and in fact did not do so in this case. Nonetheless they do, on the total evidence of this inquiry, indicate what the London adult public feels towards its Metropolitan Police Force.

Whereas the reactions of *young people* (13 to 20-year olds) are also in general quite favourable, they are less so than are those of the adult population, the main difference being in terms of the percentage who endorsed the *very* favourable rating.

While being distinctly favourable, the *police view* of how the public reacts to them appears to approximate to the reaction of 'young people' but to under-rate quite appreciably the favourableness of 'adult' reactions. The underestimate is greatest with respect to 'feeling at ease' with the police, but it applies generally to all five classes of reaction.

Quite possibly the judgments of the police are especially affected by their contact with young people, but it is also feasible that they are in general influenced by the apparent attitudes of those population sectors with which their duties call especially for contact — presumably a sector somewhat less favourably disposed towards the police than is the public generally.

Certain other reactions to the police

The police officers interviewed were also asked how they thought the public reacted to them in certain other respects, namely what proportion of the public they felt 'take the police for granted', 'don't want to be friends with the police officer off duty', 'don't want to be friendly with the police officer on duty', 'think the police are always out to get them', 'think the police are bent'.

Of these five propositions, the one most frequently endorsed (as believed held by the public) was 'they take the police for granted': 47 per cent thought this was true of 'everyone or almost everyone' and 89 per cent that it was true of at least half the London population. The position was markedly different for the other four propositions or statements, with very few police officers saying the statement was true of 'everyone or almost everyone' (not more than 3 per cent for any one statement) and a third or more saying the statement was true of 'nobody or almost nobody'. The two statements most frequently denied were that the public 'thinks the police are bent' and that the public thinks 'the police are always out to get them'.

The public's view of the character and the characteristics of officers in the Metropolitan Police Force

Adults and young people used a standard rating scale to say to what extent they felt the police had certain characteristics and the police sample used the same scale to say what *they thought* the public's opinion was in this regard.

Adult views about the characteristics of the police

Members of the adult sample used the rating scale to indicate to what extent they thought the police were friendly, rude and so on for each of a range of characteristics, namely:

Friendly	Interfering	Dishonest
Rude	Fair	Intelligent
Courteous	Calm	Distant
Frightening	Bullying	Secretive
Kind	Efficient	Well trained

They were also asked if they thought it a good or a bad thing that the police had whatever characteristics they (the adult public) attributed to them. Results are shown in Table 2.

In very general terms, there was a strong tendency for adult Londoners to endorse the characteristics 'well trained', 'calm', 'efficient', 'courteous', 'fair', 'kind', 'intelligent', 'friendly'. There was also a substantial number of people denying that the police were 'rude', 'frightening', 'interfering' or 'bullying', 'dishonest'. At a more specific level, the salient findings were as follows.

9

1 Adult Londoners see the police as friendly and are well satisfied with this. On the other hand, nearly half perceive the police as 'distant' — though the majority of these people regarded this situation as a 'good thing'.

2 About three-quarters of the public rated the police as at least 'fairly' secretive although even extreme secretiveness tended to be regarded as desirable.

3 About one in six saw the police as frightening or interfering, though the majority of these people regarded such qualities as desirable. On the other hand those who tend to see the police as being without such qualities tend also to regard that state as desirable.

Table 2

Ratings of the police in terms of various characteristics

Characteristics rated	Percentages of respondents endorsing the different rating terms											
	Adult ratings				Young people ratings				How police think the public sees them			
	Extremely or very	Fairly	Just a bit	Not at all	Extremely or very	Fairly	Just a bit	Not at all	Extremely or very	Fairly	Just a bit	Not at all
	(%)	(%)	(%)	(%)	(%)	(%)	(%)	(%)	(%)	(%)	(%)	(%)
Well-trained	85	13	1	—	82	15	1	1	74	25	—	—
Calm	80	18	2	1	*				83	17	—	—
Efficient	66	32	1	—	*				45	53	2	—
Courteous	65	31	3	1	*				44	53	2	—
Fair	63	33	3	1	46	44	8	2	63	35	1	1
Kind	55	39	4	1	40	48	11	—	41	53	5	—
Intelligent	55	42	2	1	* See 'Brainy'				13	78	7	1
Friendly	50	42	7	1	40	45	13	2	41	54	4	—
Secretive	50	28	11	7	*				42	36	17	5
Rude	2	7	29	62	6	17	42	35	1	9	69	19
Dishonest	3	10	45	40	* See 'Honest'				1	4	73	21
Interfering	5	13	31	50	* See 'Nosey'				18	22	47	11
Frightening	6	11	27	54	6	23	39	30	5	15	54	26
Bullying	6	13	38	40	16	25	41	16	2	8	62	27
Distant	12	32	26	28	*				14	37	36	12
Honest	*				53	37	8	2	*			
Brainy	*				41	48	8	2	*			
Nosey	*				32	30	26	12	*			
Sneaky	*				25	24	32	19	*			

*Sample not asked to rate on this characteristic

4 About one in five regarded the police as being at least fairly bullying, though nearly half of these people thought that this situation was 'a good thing'.

5 Thirteen per cent rated the police as appreciably 'dishonest' and forty per cent as 'not at all' dishonest.

The public's perception of the character of the police appears on this evidence to be generally supportive, to be understanding and insightful in nature, but nonetheless to involve an element of dissatisfaction or criticism. The public's views in relation to the honesty of the police are especially worth attention.

Young persons' views about the characteristics of the police

Members of the young person sample were asked similar questions, although the wording of the listed characteristics was in some ways modified to fit 'young person' thinking and experience. The nature of these differences can be seen in Table 2.

The salient indications of the young person findings were as follows:

1 The ratings of the young person sample were in general favourable. Thus, there was a clear tendency for these respondents to regard the police as at least 'fairly' friendly, brainy, fair, well trained, honest, kind. The grading was highest for 'goodness of training' with 82 per cent saying that the police were at least 'very' well trained. However, for certain other characteristics the situation was more mixed. Thus, whereas 35 per cent denied that the police are at all rude, the others attributed at least some degree of rudeness to them and 23 per cent regarded them as at least 'fairly' rude. Similarly for their being 'frightening', 'bullying'. About as many regarded the police as 'sneaky' as did not; somewhat more thought of them as 'nosy' than did not.

2 Having said this, it is important to note that with one exception, the ratings of the young person sample were consistently less favourable than the ratings of the adults.

The difference was greatest for the term 'bullying', and was also quite large for 'rudeness' and tendency to be 'frightening'. For 'well trained' (the exception) there was virtually no difference between the young person and the adult ratings.

Police opinions about how the public sees them

The police sample used the same scale to say how *they felt* the public rated them on the same characteristics, with the following results.

1 The police feel that the public rates them quite favourably in terms of all the positive-sounding characteristics in the list, in the order:* 'calm', 'well trained', 'fair', 'efficient', 'kind', 'friendly', 'courteous', 'intelligent'. They also feel that the public tends to reject the view that the police are to any substantial degree 'dishonest', 'bullying', 'rude' or 'frightening'. But this tendency breaks down with respect to the characteristics 'interfering', 'distant', 'secretive', the public being thought to attach these characteristics to the police to a fairly substantial degree.

2 Police views about how the public rates them are generally less favourable than the way the adult public does in fact feel about the police, but approximate to the views of young people.

Summing up on the public's views about the characteristics of the police

In general, then, the adult public rates the police very favourably in relation to the characteristics investigated, whereas young people, though favourably disposed, rate them less favourably. The police view of how the public feels about them approximates to the views of young people but underestimates the favourableness of the adult public's view.

*As indicated by the weighted scores, where 'extremely' = 1, 'very' = 2, 'fairly' = 3, 'just a bit' = 4, 'not at all' = 5.

2 HOW THE POLICE ARE THOUGHT TO BEHAVE IN CERTAIN SITUATIONS

Members of the adult sample were asked how they felt the police behaved in each of a range of situations, namely:

At the scene of a road accident.

At a home that has been burgled.

At a demonstration.

When bringing bad news.

When stopping a motorist for an offence.

When stopping someone in the street to search him.

When giving someone directions.

At the police station when someone comes to ask them something.

When dealing with children who have done something wrong.

On the telephone when someone phones them up to report something.

Responses could take the form of endorsement or rejection of terms such as: the police are off-hand (in that situation), . . . courteous, . . . cheerful, . . . as helpful as they can be, . . . rude.

The main indications of the responses were as follows.

1 Generally speaking, the police are rated very favourably over a range of situations differing markedly in the scope they offer for adverse reaction to the police. Descriptive terms getting a persistently high level of endorsement were courteous, efficient, helpful, tactful, fair. This type of result must be viewed against the fact that most of the situations involved were either of an abrasive nature with respect to public relations or of a traumatic or emotionally-toned kind.

2 Nonetheless, there was evidence of dissatisfaction at a minority level about police behaviour in certain of the situations investigated. These dissatisfactions were principally that police:

13

a. Fail to show gratitude when something is reported to them by telephone (16 per cent).

b. Push people around at the scene of a road accident (16 per cent).

c. Embarrass people at the scene of a house burglary (14 per cent).

d. Make people feel small if they go to the police station to ask for something (12 per cent).

e. Are inefficient in dealing with children who have done wrong (10 per cent).

f. Are unfair when stopping someone in the street to search them (9 per cent) or when stopping a motorist for an offence (9 per cent).

g. Are unfair (9 per cent), brutal (8 per cent) at demonstrations.

The reference to 'brutal' treatment of demonstrators is not, it should be noted, out of line with the evidence presented elsewhere in this report to the effect that the public tends to favour the police being quicker to arrest demonstrators.

3 CIRCUMSTANCES AND POLICE BEHAVIOUR LIKELY TO AFFECT POLICE—PUBLIC RELATIONS

Members of both the adult and the youth samples were asked to consider two sets of propositions about the police. The first set dealt with circumstances and behaviour of a kind that, while not necessarily involving police malpractice, were quite likely to work against good public relations. The second set referred directly to police malpractices. The propositions put to the young-person sample differed somewhat from those put to the adult sample, having been based on the indications of the exploratory interviews with young people.

In addition, police officers were asked for their views about the effects, on police—public relations, of certain aspects of their own working arrangements (e.g. the present method of investigating complaints against the police).

14

The views of adults and young people about police behaviour

Table 3

Level of agreement with different propositions about the police: adult sample

The views of adults

With regard to the set of propositions listed in Table 3, the respondent was asked to say of each statement whether he thought it true or false.

Proposition	Proportion agreeing (%)
The police have lost touch with people now that police drive around in cars	59
Policemen are never around when you need them	58
The newspapers are always too ready to report things that show police in a bad light	50
It depends what mood a policeman is in whether he reports a motorist or not	48
Once a person has a criminal record, the police never leave him alone	38
Policemen spend too much time doing office work and not enough time on the beat	38
It's often police on point-duty that cause the traffic jams	31
Some police go out of their way to arrest people so that they will be promoted quicker	31
Police are always too ready to side with the authorities against the ordinary person	30
The police don't investigate properly complaints made against them	25
The more expensive your car, the more likely you are to get away with motoring offences	25
Television programmes are always too ready to show the police in a bad light	23
The police can't be bothered dealing with petty crime	20

The salient features of these findings appear to be as follows.

1 All thirteen propositions were endorsed as true by a large proportion of the sample, the most frequently endorsed being 'the police have lost touch with people now that the police drive round in cars' (59 per cent) and the least frequently endorsed being 'the police can't be bothered dealing with petty crime' (20 per cent).

The other rates of endorsement are shown above and the total picture must be regarded as calling for serious attention.

2 There is a major difference in the proportion thinking that *newspapers* 'are always too ready to report things that show the police in a bad light' (50 per cent) and the proportion saying this of *television* (23 per cent).

3 The proposition that the police do not properly investigate complaints made against them was endorsed by 25 per cent of the respondents.

15

Table 4

Claimed frequency of certain kinds of malpractices and the origin of such views: adult sample

With the second set of propositions, detailed in Table 4, each respondent was required to say (a) if he or she thought the alleged behaviour ever occurred and (b) if so, how often he or she thought it occurred; (c) if so, whether he or she had ever had direct experience of that form of police behaviour and where.

Type of behaviour	Section 8, Q.2: 'Do you think this *ever* happens?'			Section 8, Q.3: 'How often do you think this happens?'						Section 8, Q.4: 'Have you ever come across this personally?'		
	Yes	No	N.I.†	Very often	Fairly often	Not very often	Hardly ever	N.I.†	Weighted mean*	Yes	No	N.I.†
	(%)	(%)	(%)	(%)	(%)	(%)	(%)	(%)	(%)	(%)	(%)	(%)
London police steal things at scenes of crimes	48	50	2	1	5	23	19	0	1.86	3	45	—
London police use unfair methods to get information	56	41	3	4	14	29	9	—	2.29	4	52	—
London police plant things on people	41	57	2	2	4	19	16	0	1.76	2	39	—
London police tell lies in court	46	51	3	3	7	22	14	0	1.94	8	38	—
London police beat people up in police stations	52	45	3	3	7	27	15	0	2.05	5	47	—
London police take bribes	67	30	3	3	7	37	20	0	2.31	5	62	—
London police use too much force when arresting people	48	50	2	3	10	26	9	—	2.05	10	38	—
London police do not allow arrested persons to get in touch with their family or solicitor	21	74	5	1	4	10	6	—	1.44	3	18	—
London police force their way into people's homes without a warrant	36	61	3	1	5	19	11	—	1.70	5	31	—
London police hush up complaints made against them	59	37	4	4	11	33	11	—	2.31	2	57	—

*Weighted mean when the following weights are given to the different responses: not at all =1; hardly ever = 2; not very often = 3; fairly often = 4; very often = 5. Hence a low mean indicates relatively few people claiming that police behave in the way indicated and a high mean indicates the opposite.

†No information available.

In this case, the more noteworthy features of the findings were as follows.

1 The number of people endorsing the various forms of behaviour as 'ever' happening is relatively high, with four of the acts getting endorsement from over 50 per cent of the sample and the lowest level of endorsement of any of them being 21 per cent. At the same time, the stipulation 'ever' is very broad and in this context it is worth noting that 74 per cent of the sample denied that the police *ever* use too much force when arresting people.

2 The kinds of behaviour said more frequently to occur include the use of unfair methods to get information (18 per cent say this happens either 'very' often or 'fairly' often), the hushing-up of complaints against the police (15 per cent), using too much force when arresting people (13 per cent).

3 Only a small minority of those claiming that the police commit the acts specified in Table 4 say that this claim is based on personal experience. The most frequently-claimed sources of their impressions were: the newspapers (especially in relation to the taking of bribes, the hushing-up of complaints), hearsay, personal assumption. Television is low in the list of claimed sources.

Table 5
Level of agreement with certain propositions about the police: youth sample

Proposition	Proportion agreeing (%)
It depends what mood a policeman is in whether he tells you off or not	59
If it's your word against a policeman's, he always wins	57
The scruffier you look, the more likely the police are to nick you	56
Policemen are never around when you need them	52
When the police search pepole in the street, they *try* to make them feel small	45
Once you've been in trouble, the police never leave you alone	43
When they are called to a noisy party, the police throw their weight around and act big	37
Some policemen make as many arrests as they can to get promoted quicker	36
Uniforms make policemen look frightening	27
Television programmes are always too ready to show the police up badly	25

Table 6

Claimed frequency of certain kinds of malpractice and origin of such views: youth sample

Statement about police behaviour	Do they ever?			If so, how often?					Come across it personally?	
	Yes	No	N.I.*	Very	Fairly	Not very	Hardly ever	N.I.*	Yes	No
	(%)	(%)	(%)	(%)	(%)	(%)	(%)	(%)	(%)	(%)
London police hush up complaints made against them	71	28	1	9	23	29	10	0	5	66
London police use unfair methods to get information	67	32	1	6	19	31	11	0	7	60
London police use too much force when arresting people	66	33	1	10	24	25	7	—	22	44
London police take bribes	62	35	2	4	11	24	23	—	2	60
London police force their way into people's homes without a warrant	58	40	2	3	11	29	15	0	5	53
London police do not let arrested persons get in touch with anyone soon enough	56	41	3	6	23	19	8	—	8	48
London police beat people up in police stations	47	51	3	8	11	15	12	—	8	37
London police tell lies in court	42	56	2	3	8	15	16	—	5	36
London police plant things on people	41	57	2	4	10	13	14	0	5	36
London police steal things at scenes of crimes	39	59	2	2	5	15	17	0	1	37

*No information available

18

The views of young people

The same kinds of propositions, suitably modified, were put to the young-person sample, with the results shown in Tables 5 and 6.

1 For the first set of these propositions, dealing with situations that could quite possibly work against good public relations, the distribution of responses was as shown in Table 5. For comparable propositions, the results are broadly similar to those obtained for the adult sample.

2 However, for the statements about police malpractice (Table 6), the youth sample claimed a substantially higher frequency of occurrence than did the adult sample, the biggest differences, proportionately speaking, being connected with propositions about the police:
a. using too much force when arresting people (34:13 per cent saying it happens very or fairly frequently);
b. hushing-up complaints made against them (32:15 per cent);
c. forcing their way into homes without a warrant (14:6 per cent);
d. planting things on people (14:6 per cent);

3 Here, too, the proportion who claimed that malpractice occurred but who had not come across an instance of it personally, was very high. Whereas for *adults*, newspapers were named most often as the source of views about police malpractices (with television far below in frequency of mention), for young people television was slightly ahead of newspapers. For both adults and young people, hearsay was also an important source of the views held.

Police views about aspects of their working arrangements and about how these bear upon relations with the public

In this same general context (i.e. of views about the effects of police behaviour and practice upon police–public relations) the members of the police-officer sample were asked to say if they agreed or disagreed with each of a range of statements about police duties which have an obvious

19

Table 7
Police views about
desirable working
arrangements

bearing upon the relations between police and public (e.g. wherever possible, police officers on duty should wear plain clothes when they visit people's homes; more police should be home-beat officers). The distribution of responses is given in Table 7.

Statement considered	Proportion agreeing (%)
The police view should be presented more forcefully in an attempt to change laws that they think are unfair or unenforceable	90
Wherever possible, police officers should live in the community rather than in section houses or groups of police homes	88
More uniformed police officers should be walking their beats instead of driving around in cars	67
Police officers should have more opportunity to take part in community activities in their off-duty hours	65
Traffic wardens should take over more of the traffic duties that the police now do*	64
It should be official practice to give women police officers more opportunity to carry out a wider range of police work	62
Every police officer doing specialized duties should be encouraged to do a period of general duties from time to time	60
Complaints against police officers should be investigated by suitably-qualified people outside the Force	38
Wherever possible, police officers on duty should wear plain clothes when they visit people's homes	30
The 'Specials' should take over more of the duties that regular police do now	6

*This statement relates to the situation at the time of the survey

Table 7 supports the following conclusions:

1 The most frequently-endorsed statement was: 'The police view should be presented more forcefully in an attempt to change laws that they think are unfair or unenforceable'.

2 There was a large measure of support for several statements to the effect that there should be greater involvement of the police in community affairs, for example

a. 'Wherever possible police officers should live in the community rather than in section houses or in groups of police houses' (88 per cent agreed).
b. 'Police officers should have more opportunity to take part in community activities in their on-duty hours (65 per cent).

20

3 Sixty per cent felt that 'officers doing special duties should from time to time be encouraged to do a period of general duties'.

4 Thirty-eight per cent endorsed the statement that 'complaints against police officers should be investigated by suitably qualified people outside the police force'; nearly 60 per cent rejected that proposition.

5 Nearly two-thirds of the police respondents agreed it 'should be official practice to give women officers more opportunity to carry out a wider range of police work'.

6 There was widespread rejection of the view that the Special Constabulary should take over more of the duties that regular police officers do now.

Table 8
Police acceptance or rejection of statements alleging police malpractice

Still broadly in the same context, police officers were asked to endorse as true or not true six statements alleging police malpractice or reactions to malpractice, as detailed in Table 8.

The statement	True (%)	Not true (%)	N.I.* (%)
The police tend to be too secretive about some aspects of their work	57	43	—
Often one of the deciding factors as to whether a police officer books a motorist is the officer's mood	29	71	—
Police officers are too ready to cover up for colleagues they know have done something wrong	26	71	3
In order to catch criminals, police are justified in providing opportunities for crime to happen	25	74	1
Once a person has a criminal record, the police never leave him alone	2	98	—
The police are the first to want to see a bent copper brought to justice	94	4	2

*No usable information

The main indications of the data in Table 8 are as follows:

1 Respondents were almost unanimous in their denial of the statement 'once a person has a criminal record the police never leave him alone', and the great majority (94

21

per cent) agreed that 'the police are the first to want to see a bent copper brought to justice'.

2 In partial contrast with these majority reactions, about a quarter of the respondents said it was true that:

a. 'Police officers are too ready to cover up for colleagues they know have done something wrong' (26 per cent); and,
b. 'Often one of the deciding factors as to whether a police officer books a motorist or not is the officer's mood' (29 per cent).

3 Still in the context of self criticism, about half the respondents thought it true that 'the police tend to be too secretive about some aspects of their work'.

4 A finding of particular interest and import is that 25 per cent of the respondents endorsed the view that 'in order to catch criminals, police are justified in providing opportunity for crime to happen'.

4 POLICE BEHAVIOUR AND ATTITUDES TOWARDS CERTAIN SUB-GROUPS IN THE POPULATION

How the police are perceived as treating certain minority groups and population sectors

Both the adult and the youth samples were asked how they felt the police behaved in relation to certain population sectors. Members of the police sample were asked for their views about which sub-groups tended most to cause them trouble.

The views of adults

The members of the adult sample were questioned in relation to each of the following sub-groups:

Motorists	Coloured people
Long-haired hippy types	Irish people
Teenagers and young people	Poor people
Demonstrators	Rich people

Table 9

Showing the percentage of adults agreeing with the propositions about police behaviour

With respect to each of these, the respondent was asked if he/she thought that the police pushed them around, picked on them, were quicker to arrest them, let them get away with things, were especially helpful to them, treated them the same as anyone else.

The results are set out in summary form in Table 9 and their principal indications are set below it.

Population sub-group or minority	Police push them around (%)	Police pick on them (%)	Police are quicker to arrest them * (%)	Police let them get away with things (%)	Police especially helpful to them* (%)	Police treat them same as everyone else* (%)
Long-haired hippy types	32	25	36	15	31	59
Demonstrators	31	15	38	22	45	59
Motorists	15	15	22	28	63	79
Teenagers and young people	13	14	17	22	58	76
Coloured people	13	11	17	16	47	74
Poor people	11	8	17	13	59	78
Irish people	9	7	13	9	33	85
General public	3	3	7	20	92	—
Rich people	1	2	4	33	49	62

*The wording of the first and the second of the marked propositions was slightly changed for the questions about 'the general public'. The third of them was not asked about 'the general public'

1 There is very considerable variation in terms of the degree to which the different population sectors are thought by the public to receive adverse attention from the police, with 32 per cent thinking the police push around the long-haired hippy types and only 1 per cent thinking this of rich people. These extremes compare with a figure of 3 per cent for the general public.

2 With respect to being regarded as receiving adverse police treatment, the other sub-groups are positioned between these two extremes, in the order: demonstrators, motorists, teenagers and young people, coloured people, poor people, Irish people. A noteworthy feature of this evidence is that coloured people are about midway in the rankings, being about on a par with young people and the poor and being better positioned than motorists and long-haired hippy types.

23

3 As seen by the adult public, the receipt of *adverse* treatment does not necessarily imply an absence of *favoured* treatment or vice versa. Thus, motorists are regarded as receiving a relatively high degree of adverse treatment, but are second only to the general public in receiving *favoured* treatment. The overall ordering of groups with respect to receipt of favoured treatment was in fact: the general public, motorists, rich people, teenagers and young people, poor people, demonstrators, coloured people, long-haired hippy types, Irish people.

4 Respondents who said they believed the police to be quicker to arrest certain groups, were asked if they thought this was a good or a bad thing. Public sympathy in this respect varied markedly from group to group, being highest for poor people and lowest for rich people, the intermediate order being: coloured people, teenagers and young people, long-haired hippy types, the Irish, motorists, the general public, demonstrators.

Public disapproval of what they perceived as a tendency of the police to let certain sub-groups 'get away with things' was greatest with respect to the rich and least with respect to the poor, the intermediate rankings being: long-haired hippy types, coloured people, demonstrators, Irish people, teenagers and young people, motorists, the general public.

Putting the evidence in Item 4 another way, it appears that:

1 Public *dis*approval of police treatment of special groups is involved when there is:

a. any tendency by the police to be quicker to arrest poor people, coloured people, teenagers and young people;
b. any tendency of the police to let the rich, the long-haired hippy types, coloured people or demonstrators . . . 'get away with things'.

2 Public *approval* of police treatment of special groups is involved when there is:

a. any tendency of the police to be quick to arrest the rich, demonstrators, members of the general public;

b. any tendency of the police to let poor people or members of the general public 'get away with things'.

In these findings, the views about the 'general public' are at first sight contradictory and this contradiction can be resolved only with the assumption that approval of their quick arrest relates to *serious* breaches of the law and that approval of the general public being allowed to 'get away with things' relates to *trivial* matters.

The views of young people

The groups about which the young-person sample provided views were to some extent different from those dealt with by the adult sample, namely,

<table>
<tr><td>Demonstrators</td><td>Young people under 21</td></tr>
<tr><td>Young coloured people</td><td>generally</td></tr>
<tr><td>Skinheads and greasers</td><td>The general public, 21 or over</td></tr>
</table>

Table 10
Showing the percentage of the youth sample agreeing with the propositions about police behaviour

The main pattern of youth responses is shown in summary form in Table 10.

Population sub-group or minority	Police push them around (%)	Police pick on them (%)	Police are quicker to arrest them (%)	Police let them get away with things (%)	Police especially helpful to them (%)	Police treat them same as everyone else (%)
Demonstrators	69	37	68	19	26	32
Skinheads and greasers	67	56	74	13	16	25
Long-haired hippy types	54	41	56	12	20	41
Young people under 21 in general	26	24	30	14	43	64
Young coloured people	21	19	20	13	34	65
Young people who drive	18	26	31	12	44	69
The general public 21 or over	5	6	10	14	70	NA*

*Not applicable

The principal indications of these data appear to be as follows:

25

1 The respondents regard skinheads and greasers, demonstrators, long-haired hippy types as being *acted against* more than others (i.e. in terms of the police pushing them around, picking on them, being quicker to arrest them).

2 On balance, somewhat fewer respondents thought young coloured people were *adversely treated* by the police than thought this of young people in general. But on the other hand, fewer thought the police were *especially helpful* to young coloured people than thought this of young people generally.

The young people in the sample were also asked if they thought it a good or a bad thing that the police treated different population sub-groups in the way they (i.e. the respondents) perceived the police as doing. Some of the main indications of their responses are as follows:

1 Respondents overwhelmingly approve of the members of any one group being treated equally with anyone else — irrespective of what the group is. (On the other evidence of this section, this 'equal treatment' appears to mean 'equally *fair* treatment'.)

2 *Adverse police treatment* (though not, presumably, *unfair* treatment) of the members of a group is regarded favourably or unfavourably according to the nature of that group. Thus, there is a tendency to regard it as a *bad* thing if the police are quicker to arrest (or tend to push around) young people generally, young coloured people, young people who drive, long-haired hippy types, but a good thing if this is done with respect to skinheads and greasers, demonstrators.

3 The position with respect to young coloured people is especially noteworthy. Respondents were against anything they interpreted as adverse police treatment of young coloured people and markedly in favour of members of this group 'being treated the same as anyone else' — though they were also against members of that group being allowed by the police 'to get away with things'.

Comparing adult and youth opinions

It is possible on the evidence available to comapre the views of London adults and young people, with the following indications:

1 Adults tended much less than young people to regard the police as dealing adversely with the sub-groups or minorities listed in the table. For example, whereas 69 per cent of the youth sample claimed the police pushed demonstrators around, the figure for the adult sample was 31 per cent; whereas 56 per cent of the youth sample claimed that the police were quicker to arrest long-haired hippy types, the figure for adults was 36 per cent.

2 For all groups considered, adults tended somewhat more than young people to regard the police as being especially helpful to members of such groups and as letting them 'get away with things'.

3 Amongst the adults and young people who agreed that the police are 'quicker to arrest' members of some group, there was greater approval of this situation by the adults than by the young people.

In other words, young people tended less than adults *both* to think of the police as being well disposed towards the groups considered and to approve when the police do take arresting action.

Police views about population sub-groups that produce problems for them and about the nature of the problems that these sub-groups cause

Each police officer in the 1,000-officer sample rated each of thirty population sub-groups in terms of whether that group caused problems for the police. Each respondent then identified the top three groups in terms of his opinion about their tendency to produce problems for the police. The results were principally as follows:

1 There was a great deal of variation between the groups in terms of the percentage of police officers rating them as sources of problems or as causing work for the police,

Table 11
Proportion of police officers who claim different sub-groups produce problems for the police

ranging from demonstrators at one extreme (with 90 per cent thus rating them) to shopkeepers at the other (9 per cent). Percentages for all thirty are given in Table 11.

Sub-group	(%)	Sub-group	(%)	Sub-group	(%)
Demonstrators	90	Indians and Pakistanis	45	Lorry drivers	19
Football fans	82	Long-haired hippy types	43	Taxi drivers	19
Drug addicts	80	Africans	43	Lawyers	19
Political extremists	75	Prostitutes	40	Stall holders	19
Juveniles (14 to 16 yrs)	73	Students	36	Tourists	18
Skinheads and greasers	72	Children (under 14 yrs)	36	Judges and magistrates	17
Private motorists	67	Delivery men	35	Old people (more than 65 yrs)	16
Vagrants	56	Irish people	28	Upper social class	12
West Indians	53	Homosexuals	28	Shopkeepers	9
Young people (17 to 24)	52	Working-class people	22	Middle-class people	9

2 For each group rated by the respondent as in the top three for tendency to cause problems, the respondent was asked if it was *all* the members of the sub-group concerned he had in mind or only some of them — and if only 'some', *which* members were the problem-producers? For most of the groups, the majority of respondents said it was only 'some' that produced problems. Over the whole range of the more troublesome groups, characteristics of the trouble-making elements were predominantly: male, working class, young. By contrast, certain characteristics and groups tended not to be singled out as trouble-producing, namely: female, upper class, Indians, Pakistanis, West Indians, Irish.*

3 Respondents were asked to specify the *kinds* of problems or work caused by groups they had named as the more prone to create problems. Certain classes of problems emerged as not only commonly perceived in relation to some *specific* group but as commonly perceived in relation to *several* groups.

a. They put a strain on available police facilities and resources (e.g. demonstrators, private motorists, drug addicts, political extremists, juveniles, football fans).

*Fieldwork was conducted before London bomb incidents.

b. They participate in rowdyism, hooliganism; deliberately create a lot of noise (e.g. football fans, juveniles, demonstrators, young people aged 17 to 24).

c. They are often involved in theft or housebreaking or robbery (e.g. juveniles, young people, drug addicts).

d. They commit many of the offences that the police have to deal with (e.g. juveniles, young people, drug addicts).

5 THE DUTIES OF THE POLICE IN THE CONTEXT OF POLICE—PUBLIC RELATIONS

In both the adult and the youth surveys, respondents were asked how well they thought the police did certain jobs ranging from catching professional criminals to helping to settle family rows. They were also asked how important they thought it was that these jobs should be *police* duties.

The views of adults and young people about the duties of the police

The views of adults

On the evidence gathered, it was possible to rank the duties in terms both of how important it is that the police do them and of *how well* the police are thought to do them. Details are given in Table 12 and comments follow it.

1 The relationship between the two rankings was relatively low. In other words, tasks that the public thought of as important police duties were not necessarily the ones that they thought the police were doing especially well.

2 Top of the list, in terms of it being important that the police do them, are the traditional key duties of the police, namely, catching professional criminals and preventing crime. Catching motorists who have been drinking is third in order but directing traffic and dealing with parking offences are well down on the list.

3 In terms of *how important* it is that the police do tasks of the kind asked about, approximately 50 per cent* of the

*Note that the figures in Table 12 relate to the percentages saying *very* important. Table 5 on p. 17 of Part 1 is the source of the reference 'approximately 50 per cent'.

Table 12
Comparing the importance
and efficiency ratings

The jobs done by police officers/that police officers might do	Proportion regarding it as 'very important' that the police do this job (%)	(R/O†)	Proportion saying the police do this job 'very well' (%)	(R/O §)
Catching professional criminals	98	(1)	46	(8)
Preventing crime	94	(2)	39	(11)
Protecting people who have been threatened by someone	86	(4)	48	(5)
Catching motorists who have been drinking	81	(3)	36	(12)
Controlling crowds at demonstrations	79	(5)	81	(2)
Helping people who are lost, stranded or ill	77	(6)	83	(1)
Catching people who take drugs	70	(8)	31	(14)
Dealing with children who break the law	65	(10)	44	(9)
Controlling crowds at football matches	64	(9)	65	(3)
Getting back stolen property	63	(7)	24	(17)
Directing traffic*	60	(13)	69	(4)
Advising motorists about their driving	55	(11)	42	(10)
Catching people who steal things that are not worth much	43	(12)	26	(16)
Talking to children who won't go to school	29	(17)	33	(7)
Stopping a play or a film that may be immoral	27	(16)	18	(18)
Helping to run things like youth clubs	21	(15)	24	(13)
Dealing with parking offences*	20	(14)	49	(6)
Helping to settle family rows	13	(18)	23	(15)

*These questions were asked prior to the main period of change with respect to these duties.
†Rank order is based on total distribution, where 'very important' = 1, 'fairly' = 2, 'not very' = 3, 'not at all' = 4, 'not a job for the police at all' = 5. The rank order of weighted scores does not, therefore, necessarily tally with the rank order based solely upon the percentage saying 'very important'.
§ Rank order is based on the total distribution where 'very well' = 1, 'fairly well' = 2, 'not very well' = 3, 'badly' = 4.

respondents did not see it as important that the police should be the ones to: help settle family rows, help run things like youth clubs, talk to children who won't go to school, stop plays or films that may be immoral. By contrast, at least 80 per cent felt it was 'very important' that the police should be engaged in catching professional criminals, in preventing crime, in protecting people who have been threatened, in catching motorists who have been drinking.

4 In terms of *how well* the police do the eighteen jobs asked about, the top ranking is for 'helping people who are lost or stranded or ill', and the lowest is for 'stopping a play or film that may be immoral'. Crowd control is well up in the list, but catching professional criminals is only eighth and 'getting back stolen property' is almost at the bottom of the list.

5 At the same time it is important to note that there was no task amongst the eighteen that was rated below 'fairly well' by more than 30 per cent of the respondents.

6 Respondents who said that certain jobs should *not* be done by the police were asked to explain why they thought this. The more commonly given reasons were to the effect that:

a. Police are needed to deal with crime and already have enough to do without having to attend to things like family quarrels, children who won't go to school, stopping entertainment that may be immoral, helping to run youth clubs.
b. The police are not qualified to do the tasks concerned (e.g. dealing with family quarrels, talking to children who won't go to school) and would be ineffective at it.
c. Morality is not the concern of the police.
d. The presence of the police could worsen the situation, upset the people involved, evoke the disrespect that young people have for the police.
e. This duty is the responsibility of the people directly concerned (e.g. as in family rows).

The preferred agencies for doing the 'unsuitable' tasks are given in the main report.

The views of young people

Just as for the adult survey, the members of the youth sample rated certain jobs in terms both of how well the police did them and of how important it was that the *police* should be the ones to do them. These ratings are summarized in Table 13.

31

Table 13

Comparing the importance and the efficiency ratings for a range of duties: youth sample

1 One of the clear indications of the data in Table 13 is that the relationship between the two sets of ratings is by no means high. In other words, jobs that young people think are very important for the police to do are not

The jobs done by the police/that police might do	Proportion regarding it as 'very important job for the police to do' (%)	(R/O†)	Proportion saying that the police do this job 'very well' (%)	(R/O§)
Catching big crooks like bank robbers	86	(1)	35	(6)
Telling children about kerb drill and road safety	75	(2)	57	(2)
Catching people who take drugs	63	(3)	26	(10)
Getting back things that have been pinched	50	(4)	17	(12)
Keeping an eye on gangs of young people	47	(4)	30	(8)
Helping people who are lost or ill	54	(4)	62	(1)
Dealing with children who break the law	56	(7)	33	(7)
Controlling crowds at football matches	53	(8)	46	(4)
Dealing with demonstrators	49	(8)	44	(5)
Directing traffic	56	(10)	49	(3)
Stopping people who break the speed limit	32	(11)	33	(9)
Catching people who steal things that aren't worth much	26	(12)	23	(11)
Helping to run things like youth clubs	14	(13)	13	(13)
Helping to settle family rows	8	(14)	8	(14)

†Rank order is based on total distribution, where 'very important' = 1, 'fairly' = 2, 'not very' = 3, 'not at all' = 4, 'not a job for the police at all' = 5. The rank order of weighted scores does not, therefore, tally with the rank order based solely upon the percentage saying 'very important'.
§Rank order is based on the total distribution, where 'very well' = 1, 'fairly well' = 2, 'not very well' = 3, 'badly' = 4.

necessarily the ones that they think the police do very well. This, of course, had been broadly the result for the adult sample too. But particularly noteworthy in Table 13 is the evidence that:

a. 'Catching big crooks like bank robbers' is rated top as a job for the police to do, but sixth in terms of how well it is done.
b. 'Catching people who take drugs' is rated third as a job for the police to do and tenth in terms of how well it is done.
c. 'Getting back things that have been pinched' is rated fourth as a job for the police to do but twelfth in terms of how well they do it.

32

d. 'Directing traffic' is tenth in order as a job that the police should do, but third in terms of how well they do it.

2 In terms of how important it is that the police should be the ones to do certain tasks, over 50 per cent did not see it as important that the police should be the ones to help run youth clubs or to help settle family rows. By contrast, over 80 per cent felt that it was 'very' important that the police should be engaged in 'catching big crooks like bank robbers', and over 60 per cent that they should be engaged in 'telling children about kerb drill and road safety' and in 'catching people who take drugs'.

3 In terms of *how well* the police do the listed tasks, the outstanding finding is that for twelve of the fourteen tasks, a large majority say that the police do them either fairly well or very well, the following being especially noteworthy:

a. Helping people who are lost or ill (95 per cent).
b. Directing traffic (87 per cent).
c. Telling children about kerb drill and road safety (87 per cent).
d. Catching big crooks like bank robbers (85 per cent).

By contrast, less than 50 per cent regarded the following as being done at least fairly well: 'helping to run things like youth clubs' (47 per cent); 'helping to settle family rows' (45 per cent).

4 Respondents who said that certain jobs should not be done by the police were asked why they thought this. The more commonly-given views were:

a. The police have enough to do as it is/have more important things to do (given principally in relation to helping to settle family rows, helping to run things like youth clubs, directing traffic).
b. This job is the responsibility of the individuals concerned (given principally in relation to helping to settle family rows).
c. The police are not qualified or trained for this job (given principally in relation to helping to settle family rows, helping to run things like youth clubs).

d. The police are needed primarily to deal with crime, to prevent crime (given principally in relation to directing traffic, helping to run things like youth clubs, helping to settle family rows).

A comparison was made of the views of young people and adults about the importance of the police doing ten of the fourteen listed jobs and about how well they do them. (The exclusion of 'catching big crooks like bank robbers'/ 'catching professional criminals' arose out of the form of the statement differing for the adults and young persons.)

1 *Concerning how well the jobs are done.* For the ten duties involved in this comparison, there is a fairly close similarity between the rank ordering of duties (on the basis of adult and youth responses). But the percentages saying the police do jobs 'at least fairly well' are generally lower for young people than for adults.

2 *Concerning how important it is that the police do the listed jobs.* Whereas the listed jobs tend to be ranked similarly by young people and by adults, there are several noteworthy differences. Thus, young people put 'catching people who take drugs' top of the list of *ten*, compared with fourth for adults; adults put 'dealing with demonstrators' first of the list of ten, whereas young people put it fifth.

6   THE POWERS OF THE POLICE

Both adults and young people, and the police, were asked a range of questions about police powers.

The views of adults and young people about police powers

The views of adults

Adult respondents were asked if they thought the police had too much power, not enough power or just about the right amount of power. They were then asked to say in what ways the police had too much or too little power.

Findings were principally as follows:

1 Six per cent felt that the police had too much power, 32 per cent not enough, and 64 per cent answered 'about right'.

2 Among the seventy-one persons who felt the police have too much power, the examples more frequently volunteered were: the power to stop and search people; arrest people without reason or warrant; the power to enter and search a house without reason or warrant; the power to get a warrant or to prosecute on the basis solely of their own word; the court's acceptance of the word of a policeman as being more trustworthy than that of a member of the public.

3 Among the 389 people who thought the police did not have enough power, the examples most frequently volunteered were: the police should be able to stop and search a person without a warrant; the police should be able to enter/search a building without a warrant; they are not sufficiently active or forceful*, they are not able to use sufficient force at demonstrations; they have to be too cautious because of the possibility of complaints.

4 Some 47 per cent endorsed the statement: "If a policeman sees someone doing something wrong, he can choose whether to ignore it or not", and 31 per cent out of the 47 per cent regarded this as a 'good thing'. Similarly, 55 per cent of the sample endorsed the statement: "The police can decide when to take people to court and when not to", with 47 per cent out of the 55 per cent regarding this as a 'good thing'.

5 There was evidence of considerable misunderstanding of what the powers of the police actually are.

The views of young people

Young people were asked the same questions as were put to the members of the adult sample, with the following results.

*Many respondents have misunderstood or have put a wide interpretation upon the term 'power'.

1 Nineteen per cent thought the police had too much power, 28 per cent thought that the police had too little power, 52 per cent thought that the present powers of the police were about right. These figures compare with 6, 32 and 64 per cent for adults. In other words, the adult population is somewhat more satisfied than is the youth population with present powers and substantially fewer adults feel that the police have too much power (6:19 per cent).

2 The views of young people about the ways in which the police have too much power indicate a great deal of confusion about the nature of police power. Specifically, many of the volunteered 'ways' in which the police have too much power turn out to be: references to *abuses* of present powers; a view that the police do not give sufficient consideration to the feelings of the public in carrying out their duties; a view that the courts favour the police when it comes to accepting evidence. There were also errors about what the legal powers of the police actually are.

3 In listing ways in which the police should have *more* power, there were references indicating that respondents interpreted police power as police *strength* (e.g. they do not have enough power because they are undermanned). Apart from this, there was recurrent reference to things like :

a. Power to enter and search without a warrant.
b. Power to arrest on suspicion; to hold a suspect without evidence.
c. Power to stop and search motorists at random; power to enforce breathalyser tests.
d. More power to act in specific situations, such as dealing with demonstrators, drunks, vandals, vagrants.

Comparing adult and youth views

On the preceding evidence: (*a*) young people tend much more than adults to claim that the police have too much power, fewer feel that they do not have enough power, and fewer are satisfied with the present powers of the police; (*b*) the different ways in which police are thought to have too much power or too little power are not markedly

36

different for the youth and adult samples, but the youth sample is very much more prone than the adult sample to be in error of some kind about what the legal powers of the police actually are.

The views of the police about police powers

Members of the police sample were asked, with respect to each of eleven situations, if they thought that 'police on the ground' had too much power, too little power, or about the right amount of power. Those indicating that the police should have more or less power in a given situation were asked to specify the nature of the change/s they felt was/were needed. The results of this sequence of questions are set out below.

Table 14

The adequacy of police powers in certain situations: police sample

1 For ten out of the eleven situations studied, a majority of the respondents felt that present powers were 'about right'. In this respect the different situations were ranked as follows:

	Proportion saying that		
Powers relating to	Present powers are about right (%)	They want more power (%)	They want less power (%)
'Stop-and-search' procedures	82	18	—
Access to public places	79	20	1
Dealing with drunken drivers	74	25	1
Making an arrest	72	28	—
Searching suspects' homes	70	30	—
Solving civil disputes	66	8	24
Allowing or banning demonstrations	64	34	2
Dealing with children who break the law	64	30	5
Enforcing obscenity laws	58	33	8
Dealing with juveniles who break the law	57	39	4
Enforcing payment of fines	48	33	16

2 In terms of the minority wanting changes in police powers, the nature of the desired change is, in all but one situation, an *increase* in police powers. The exception is 'solving civil disputes' where there is a marked tendency amongst the dissatisfied officers to want less power.

3 The suggested changes volunteered by officers were highly varied in character, but the more recurrent of them were those which are set out in **a** and **b** below. However, in interpreting these suggestions, it is essential to bear it in mind that there was an overall tendency of a substantial kind for officers to feel that the powers of the police are about right.

a. The more frequently-volunteered classes of suggestion concerning *increased* powers were as follows:

i. 'Make the law in certain respects more rigorous and punishment more severe' (379 references to various situations, especially: enforcing obscenity laws; dealing with juveniles and children who break the law; dealing with drunken drivers).

ii. 'Give police officers greater freedom, in certain situations, to stop and search people or to search buildings at their own discretion' (206 references to various situations especially: searching suspects' homes; 'stop-and-search' operations).

iii. 'Give to police officers the power to take on-the-spot action in relation to certain kinds of offence' (188 references to various situations, especially: enforcing obscenity laws; allowing or banning demonstrations; dealing with juveniles and children who break the law).

iv. 'Certain of the rules regarding arrest, cautioning, charging should be modified into more workable forms or abolished' (158 references to various situations, especially: 'when making an arrest').

v. 'Give police greater powers to aid them in enforcing payment of fines' (111 references).

vi. 'Give to the police the power to prevent or to control demonstrations that they believe will be violent or disruptive in some way' (197 references).

b. The most frequently-volunteered class of suggestion concerning *reduced* powers was that: 'The police should not have to carry out the duty asked about' (e.g. solve civil disputes, enforce payment of fines, enforce obscenity laws (158 references)). Such tasks should instead be dealt with by the existing courts or magistrates (62 references) or the persons directly involved in the dispute (40 references) or other persons or authorities (80 references).

38

7 THE SOCIAL PHILOSOPHY OF POLICE OFFICERS AND THEIR VIEWS ABOUT THE PUBLIC

Social philosophy of police officers in relation to society generally

Police officers considered a series of propositions, each involving some aspect of social philosophy. They rated each as true or not true. The distribution of their responses is set out in Table 15.

The main indications of Table 15 are as follows:

1 There are three statements that the great majority of the respondents rejected, namely:

a. People make friends only because friends are likely to be useful to them.
b. Only when people have got what they want in life should they concern themselves with the injustices of the world.
c. No one should be punished for breaking a law that he thinks is immoral.

Table 15
Showing level of acceptance of propositions bearing on one's social philosophy: police sample

Propositions	Proportions of officers saying the propositions is		
	True (%)	Not true (%)	N.I.* (%)
Society is constantly threatened by a minority dedicated to its overthrow	51	45	—
If it weren't for youthful rebellion, there would be less progress in the world	40	60	1
The ordinary citizen really can have an influence on government decisions	39	61	—
The ideal society is one where everybody has his place and accepts it	32	67	1
People make friends only because friends are likely to be useful to them	14	86	—
No one should be punished for breaking a law that he thinks is immoral	6	93	1
Only when people have got what they want in life should they concern themselves with the injustices of the world	5	95	—

*No usable information

The rejection of the first two statements suggests a relatively non-cynical view of certain aspects of social behaviour. The large-scale rejection of the third proposition is what one might well expect in a law enforcement body (and perhaps the most interesting aspect of this finding is that 6 per cent *accepted* the statement). Nonetheless, the 93 per cent rejection does in its own right indicate a widespread strictness of outlook in this regard.

2 Responses to the other statements were much more divided in character and some of them call for special comment.

a. Sixty-one per cent rejected the view that 'the ordinary citizen really can have an influence on government decisions', and it seems important to ask if this evidence contradicts the earlier conclusion of non-cynicism or if it indicates a certain realism of outlook amongst a large number of officers.
b. Another finding which is challenging in the same sort of way is the acceptance by half the police respondents of the view that 'society is constantly threatened by a minority dedicated to its overthrow'. Does this imply an unhealthy suspiciousness on the part of the 51 per cent agreeing . . . or does it mean that policemen, in answering this question, were thinking of the criminal element and/or those revolutionary elements in society with whose activities their police duties bring them into contact? In the latter case, may one perhaps interpret the result as indicating realism? It is not possible to decide the matter on the present evidence, though that evidence does indicate the presence of an issue of importance.
c. About a third of the sample agreed that 'the ideal society is one where everyone has his place and accepts it', and this may reasonably be thought of as supportive of the *status quo* — though two-thirds of the sample rejected that view.
d. The position is equally mixed with regard to the view that 'if it weren't for youthful rebellion, there would be less progress in the world'. The rejection of this view by nearly six in ten of the respondents seems to provide further evidence of a regard for the *status quo* by a substantial part of the Force — though it may be that some of these

respondents are objecting to the 'youth' element in the statement.

What all this comes to is evidence of considerable variation in social outlook in going from officer to officer in the Metropolitan Police Force (especially with respect to the level of officers' realism, suspiciousness, attachment to the established system), but with the existence nonetheless of an over-riding outlook of non-cynicism and of strictness.

Police views about the character of the public

Table 16

Police ratings of the public's characteristics

Closely related to the social philosophy of police officers is the question of how they regard or judge the general public. Police officers were asked to rate the public in terms of a range of different characteristics, with the results shown in Table 16.

Characteristic	Extremely (%)	Very (%)	Fairly (%)	Just a bit (%)	Not at all (%)	N.I.* (%)
Friendly	—	11	54	28	6	—
Kind	1	8	57	28	6	—
Honest	—	9	74	15	2	—
Reliable	—	5	67	22	6	1
Violent	—	2	13	58	26	—
Suspicious	1	15	31	46	6	—
Apathetic	4	26	42	25	2	1
Selfish	4	34	36	25	1	—

*No usable information

In very general terms, it does appear that the police tend to regard the public as at least 'fairly' honest, reliable, friendly and kind to each other, as fairly non-violent, as fairly selfish and apathetic and as somewhat suspicious of each other.

An analysis was also made of the way in which the police judged different degrees of suspiciousness in the public (i.e. towards each other). The principal indications of this analysis were as follows:

1 There was a greater tendency for those police officers who gave the public *lower* ratings for suspiciousness (i.e. 'fairly', 'just a bit', 'not at all') *to say that this is a good*

41

thing ... than was the case for police officers who rated the public *higher* for suspiciousness (i.e. 'very', 'extremely'). Thus, over 70 per cent of those who rated the public as only 'a bit' suspicious towards each other or 'not at all' suspicious say that this is a good thing, compared with about 40 per cent for those saying that members of the public are 'very' suspicious of each other.

2 At the same time, it is noteworthy that a rating of 'very' suspicious should be regarded as a good thing by about four out of ten of the officers so rating the public. This is in line with the findings for the public's rating of the police for 'secretiveness'.

Social philosophy in relation to specific groups of people

Table 17
Level of endorsement by police officers of propositions reflecting social philosophy in relation to specific sections of the population

The study of the social outlook of police officers was taken a step further through the endorsement or rejection of a series of propositions about different sections of society (e.g. 'children nowadays have no respect for authority', 'immigrants should be obliged to adopt the British way of life', 'meths drinkers got where they are through their own fault'). Their responses are presented in Table 17.

Proposition	Proportion saying the proposition is true (%)
Criminals get off with sentences that are too light	87
Drug addicts have got where they are through their own fault	70
Users of soft drugs should be dealt with just as severely as users of hard drugs	70
Immigrants should be obliged to adopt the British way of life	66
Demonstrators are not committed to the causes for which they demonstrate	63
Meths drinkers have got where they are through their own fault	63
Motorists think that they own the road	62
People who sexually assault children deserve corporal punishment	61
Children nowadays have no respect for authority	43
Coloured people are less intelligent than whites	32
Practising homosexuals should be severely punished	13
People with long hair and hippy clothes are over-permissive and immoral	10
Irish immigrants are troublemakers*	9
Women are inferior to men	8

*Study conducted before London bomb incidents

42

Specially noteworthy features of Table 17 appear to be as follows:

1 The statements about drug addicts and 'meths drinkers' getting that way *through their own fault* were both endorsed by about two-thirds of the officers interviewed.

2 There was a very considerable degree of rejection of the statement that 'people with long hair and hippy clothes are over-permissive and immoral' and of the statement that 'practising homosexuals should be severely punished'. Of the latter statement, the possibility exists, of course, that the high rejection rate stems at least partly from the use of the term 'severely'.

3 Another of the statements that were rejected by the great majority was 'women are inferior to men'. It should be noted that some of the officers endorsing this statement qualified their endorsement of it by saying that they meant 'in some ways'.

4 About a third of the officers endorsed the statement that 'coloured people are less intelligent than whites'. It is important in this context to be aware of the distinction that is often made, by psychologists and others, in comparing different cultural groups in terms of intelligence. This distinction is between potential or innate intelligence and operational intelligence — the point being that a given class or group may well be operating below its intrinsic intelligence level because of a lack of educational or other opportunity. In the circumstances, perhaps the more important point here is that two-thirds of the respondents *rejected* the statement.

5 Three of the statements concerned the degree of punishment which should be meted out to offenders and in all three cases the majority of the respondents supported the imposition of sentences of a severe or more severe kind. Thus, 87 per cent felt that criminals at present get off with sentences that are too light; 70 per cent felt that users of soft drugs should be dealt with just as severely as users of hard drugs; 61 per cent felt that people who sexually assault children deserve corporal punishment.

6 There was also a statement about punishment of homosexuals and, seemingly in contrast with their other views about punishment, the great majority of the respondents (84 per cent) rejected the statement that 'practising homosexuals should be severely punished'.

The findings reported in Table 17 suggest a composite outlook that has in it many different and conflicting elements. Clearly present is a certain strictness and conservatism, though these aspects of outlook appear to vary with the matter concerned, being distinctly liberal for some officers in relation to certain issues. There appear also to be substantial realist and humanitarian elements tempering strictness of outlook.

8 THE PUBLIC'S WILLINGNESS TO CONTACT AND HELP THE POLICE

Public helpfulness towards the police was studied from several viewpoints: the views of both adults and young people about contacting and about helping the police, and the views of police officers themselves about the public's helpfulness.

The attitudes and behaviour of the adult Londoner in relation to helping the police

Members of the adult sample were asked about the situations in which they would *contact* the police and about their attitudes towards *helping* the police.

Contacting the police

There is an important sense in which contacting the police is a form of helping the police — in that contacting them may provide the police with information on which they can usefully act. Respondents were asked if they would contact the police in each of a range of situations (e.g. 'if you saw some teenagers damaging a telephone kiosk'). If unwilling to do so, they were asked to say why they were unwilling. Results were principally as follows:

1 There was much variation in the public's willingness to contact the police as between different situations.

	%
If your home was burgled	99
If a child of yours was lost	99
If you saw teenagers damaging a telephone kiosk	80
If you were the only person to see a car accident	80
If you lost your purse or wallet	75
If a stranger made an indecent suggestion to you	60
If you saw a stranger hanging around for a long time in your street	58
If you knew someone had a gun that he had not got a licence for	48
If you knew one of your neighbours was driving a stolen car	46
If you saw a fight in a cafe	39
If you knew someone was selling something that had been pinched	33

2 Reasons for being unwilling to contact the police were principally that the respondent felt:

a. It is somehow wrong or unfair to report people to the police.
b. There might be retaliation by the person reported.
c. No useful purpose would be served because the police are too busy or would not be interested or the trouble would be over before the police arrived.
d. The incident was not important enough or 'happens all the time'.

3 The reasons offered for not reporting a stranger hanging around for a long time in your street were principally that this person might be innocent, that the respondent did not want to get involved, and that it is not an offence.

Helping the police

Questions were asked about willingness to help the police and about the respondent's reasons for his willingness or unwillingness to do so. Following this the interviewer called out a series of different ways in which people might help the police (e.g. reporting something you have had stolen, helping at the scene of an accident, appearing in court as a witness in a police case), and asked the respondent (*a*) if he had ever helped in that way and (*b*) how willing he would be in the future to do so if the occasion for it arose. After this, the interviewer introduced a set of statements about giving evidence in court and asked the respondent to say of each if he agreed or disagreed (e.g. 'I would not want to give evidence in court because it takes up too much time'). Finally, the respondent was taken through a further set of statements, this set expressing between them different reasons for not helping the police (e.g. 'If you've helped the police, they get to know you and never leave you alone').

The results from this sequence of questions, put to members of the adult public, were broadly as follows:

1 The great majority (97 per cent) claimed that, given a chance, they would be helpful to the police, 58 per cent saying 'very helpful'.

2 Reasons for being willing to help were principally: that it is one's duty as a citizen; a belief that law and order should be maintained; that help is a two-way affair and is in one's own interests; that the police deserve help and need it to do their job. The principal reason for a negative reply was really a form of reservation, the respondent saying that it depended upon the seriousness of the situation.

3 The more frequently-offered views of the adult sample about how to increase the helpfulness of the public were: the public should be told more about the functions and duties and achievements of the police and about how they can help the police; the public should be shown that it is in their own interest to support law and order; children should be taught not to be afraid of the police but to see them as friends; the police should have more contact with the public; police behaviour and manner must be such as will invite and maintain public helpfulness; measures should be taken to reduce the present drawbacks of helping the police (e.g. lack of confidentiality, lack of protection, loss of time and earnings).

Suggestions for implementing such measures do not throw up any new approaches, but serve to indicate those likely to be more acceptable to the public (i.e. through the mass media, through police on the beat, through education and school visits, through social contacts). Furthermore, the suggested agency of change was overwhelmingly 'the police' themselves.

4 In terms of specific forms of help provided in the past, there was much variation in terms of the frequencies with which different kinds of help were said to have been given, with 64 per cent claiming that they had at some time told their children to look on the police as their friends and 1 per cent saying that they have reported a motorist for going through a red light. These and other figures are given in Table 18.

Table 18

Summarizing claims about past help to the police and about willingness to help police in the future: adult sample

Types of help	Have helped in past (%)	How willing to help in the future*			
		Very willing (%)	Fairly willing (%)	Not particularly willing (%)	Not willing at all (%)
Telling children to look on the police as their friends	64	84	13	2	1
Reporting something you have had stolen	37	82	14	2	1
Answering questions for the police during an enquiry	34	66	28	4	2
Helping at the scene of an accident	21	71	23	4	2
Asking the police to keep an eye on your home while you are away	21	55	23	15	6
Appearing in court as a witness in a police case	17	42	40	12	5
Reporting someone who you believe is about to commit a crime	10	52	34	10	3
Reporting a disturbance in a house nearby	9	36	34	21	8
Reporting a disturbance in the street	9	40	37	17	5
Helping a policeman when he is in a dangerous situation	2	50	37	9	3
Reporting a motorist for going through a red traffic light	1	23	26	31	19

*Excluding 'no information' cases

Table 18 also presents the percentages expressing *willingness* to give these same forms of help in the future and this evidence suggests that major success in getting the public's help on a wide front might well be secured if the right kinds of promotion and education were undertaken.

At the same time there is evidence of many people being less than willing to give *certain kinds* of help: reporting a motorist who goes through a red light; reporting a disturbance in a house nearby or in the street; appearing in court as a witness in a police case; helping a policeman in a dangerous situation; reporting someone you believe is about to commit a crime; asking the police to keep an eye on your home while you are away.

5 Reasons for *not* being willing to help in specified ways were numerous and the more recurrently given of them were in terms of: not wanting to be bothered or to get involved; feeling the offence is not serious; fear of consequences; waste of time because of own or police ineffectiveness; belief that the police would be uninterested or would feel inconvenienced.

The adult sample-members were also asked to rate as true or not true a number of statements presented as arguments for not helping or reporting to the police. These statements and the percentages of people who rated them 'true' are given in Table 19.

Table 19
Whether certain statements relating to helpfulness towards the police are thought to be true: adult sample

Statement	Proportion saying true (%)
The police get fed up with people who come to them over trivial things	57
When you report something to the police, you have to give your name even if you don't want to	72
A lot of crimes aren't likely to be solved, so it's not much use telling the police about them	22
If you report a crime, the police cannot protect you from the criminal getting his own back	42
You never get any thanks from the police for helping them	14
The police don't tell us enough about *how* we can help them	68
You can't trust people who give information to the police	26
If the police came to my door, my neighbours would wonder what I'd done wrong	67
It's the public's job to report people to the police, even for trivial offences	51
Some people don't 'have a go' because there is a danger of getting badly hurt	92
Some offenders get such light sentences, it's a waste of time to report them to the police	59
Some people would only report children to the police if it was very serious	84
People who go to the help of the police often end up by getting arrested themselves	14
There are some things I wouldn't report to the police, because I might do the very same thing myself	50
Some people would not help the police because they might get their name in the papers	80
If you've helped the police, they get to know you and never leave you alone	10
Sometimes people would like to help the police, but they feel they can't do anything on their own	81

The attitudes and the behaviour of young Londoners in relation to contacting/helping the police

Just as in the adult study, young people were asked about the circumstances in which they would contact the police and about their willingness to help the police.

Contacting the police

Respondents were asked with respect to each of a number of different situations if they would tell anyone about it straightaway (e.g. if you found a bunch of keys in the street, if you knew someone who had pinched a car). If they said 'yes', they were to be asked to say *who* they would tell and this question was probed to see if such persons included the police. Also, for the first four situations of which the respondent claimed he would *not* tell anyone in authority, he was asked to say *why*. Finally, the respondent was asked to say what he would do if he had lost his way and there was a policeman about and, in the event of his not being willing to ask the policeman for help, why he was unwilling to do so.

The main indications of the responses were as follows:

1 The percentage willing to contact the police did not rise beyong 68 per cent for any of the ten situations considered. Furthermore, it was well below 50 per cent with respect to 'if someone had drugs on them' (30 per cent), 'if someone

Table 20

Willingness to contact anyone/the police in different situations: youth sample

	Proportion willing to contact	
	The police (%)	Anyone (%)
If a gang of boys was beating someone up	68	87
If there was a car accident and someone got hurt	66	99
If you found a bunch of keys in the street	64	84
If some boys were breaking up a telephone kiosk	59	73
If something of yours was stolen	58	92
If you lost your purse or wallet	57	85
If someone you know had pinched a car	46	58
If someone was hanging around some parked cars	32	38
If someone had drugs on them	30	43
If a strange man followed you home at night	22	74

was hanging around some parked cars' (32 per cent), 'if a strange man followed you home at night' (22 per cent).

2 In general, the percentage of young people willing to report the specified situations to the *police* is lower than the percentage willing to report them to at least 'someone'. For some of the situations it is *markedly* lower: 'if a strange man followed you home at night', 'if something of yours was stolen', 'if there was a car accident and someone got hurt', 'if you lost your purse or wallet'.

3 Especially noteworthy is the finding that only 43 per cent would tell *anyone* in the event of their knowing someone had drugs on him.

4 Reasons volunteered for being unwilling to contact anyone were principally that the respondent felt:

a. The individual/s directly concerned should deal with the matter (offered principally in relation to reporting someone who has drugs on him).
b. It is not up to the *respondent* to do anything about it (offered principally in relation to 'if someone you knew had pinched a car', 'if boys were smashing up a telephone kiosk', 'if someone had drugs on him', 'if someone was hanging around some parked cars').
c. You cannot be sure that the suspect was in fact preparing to commit a crime (referred principally in relation to 'if you saw someone hanging around some parked cars').
d. I would not want to get someone else into trouble (e.g. 'if you knew someone had pinched a car', 'if someone had drugs on them').
e. It's too trivial to report (e.g. 'if a strange man followed you home late at night', 'if someone was hanging around parked cars').

5 Eighty-four per cent said they *would* ask the policeman the way if they were lost and another 14 per cent said that they might.

Helping the police

In the context of giving help to the police, the questions asked were closely similar to those asked of the adult sample. First of all, the respondent was asked how willing he or she would be in general to help the police and then to explain the choice of answer made and to say what he or she thought should be done to make people more helpful to the police. After this the respondent was asked how willing or otherwise he would be to answer questions for the police during an investigation and, in the event of his being less than willing, to say why. Similar questions were asked with respect to the respondent's willingness to appear in court as a witness in a police case. Finally, the respondent was offered a set of ten statements expressing between them different reasons for not helping the police and was asked to indicate which of them were true for him and which not.

The main findings were as follows:

1 The great majority (91 per cent) claimed that, given a chance, they would be helpful to the police and 47 per cent said 'very' helpful. This finding presents young people as only slightly less helpfully disposed towards the police than were adults (97 per cent helpful, with 58 per cent saying 'very' helpful).

2 Reasons volunteered by young people for being willing to help the police were principally:

a. that the respondent knows the police need the public's help in order to do their job, that the police deserve help because of the toughness of the police job;
b. a sense of duty as a citizen; belief in law and order;
c. self interest in the sense that helping the police is helping oneself.

3 Reasons volunteered for being less than helpfully disposed towards the police were principally that:

a. The police are not very helpful themselves.
b. It depends on the situation (i.e. upon how serious it is, upon whether the respondent thinks the police should be brought into the matter, whether the family or friends of

51

the respondent are likely to be involved, whether help is actually asked for by the police, whether there is risk of retaliation).

4 Respondents made various suggestions about how the police could increase the amount of help given them by young people and these suggestions included:

a. People should be better informed about police duties and methods.
b. There should be greater personal contact of a friendly kind between young people and the police.

5 Of the 503 respondents, 89 per cent said they would be willing to answer questions for the police during an investigation and 73 per cent that they would be willing to appear in court 'as a witness in a police case'. The figures for being 'very' willing were respectively 43 and 29 per cent. Adults claimed a substantially higher degree of willingness to help in these ways than did young people (i.e. 66 and 42 per cent were 'very willing' versus 43 and 29 per cent).

Table 21

Percentage of young people endorsing views that seem to bear on helpfulness towards the police: youth sample

6 Respondents were asked to consider each of ten statements about the police, each of a kind seemingly working against young people giving help to the police. Results are as follows:

	Proportion who said 'yes' (%)
Some people would not help the police, because they might get their name in the paper	75
The police don't tell us enough about *how* we can help them	68
When you report something to the police, you have to give your name even if you don't want to	64
There are some things I wouldn't report to the police, because I might do the very same thing myself	59
If you report a crime, the police cannot stop the criminal getting his own back	55
People wouldn't want to be friends with me if I told the police things	47
The police only bother about things that *they* think are important	44
The thought of going into a police station scares me	32
You never get any thanks from the police for helping them	19
If you've helped the police, they never leave you alone	18

Especially noteworthy is the view of 68 per cent of the young people that the police do not tell them enough about *how* they can help the police.

The tendency of adults to endorse the listed statements was much the same as for young people.

Public helpfulness as seen by the police

Members of the police sample rated the public on a five-point scale in terms of their helpfulness to the police. They then rated specific sections of the public in the same way (e.g. shopkeepers, Irish people, taxi drivers). They gave their reasons for judging as they did. They also rated the public's helpfulness in certain situations.

Helpfulness considered generally

The police ratings were on the usual five-point scale ranging from 'very' helpful to 'not at all' helpful. Eighty-one per cent of the officers rated the public as at least 'fairly' helpful, with 23 per cent saying they were 'very' helpful. Only 1 per cent rated them as 'not at all' helpful. At the same time, it is noteworthy that the public (both adults and young people) rates its own helpfulness even higher than this.

Police views about the helpfulness of different groups in the public

Table 22

The seven groups rated by police as most helpful and the seven rated as least helpful: police sample

Each of twenty-three selected sub-groups of the population was rated on the same five-point scale of willingness to help the police. Table 22 below lists the seven sub-groups which

	Proportion saying 'very' or 'fairly' helpful (%)		Proportion saying 'not particularly' or 'not at all' helpful (%)
Old people (over 65)	93	Skinheads and greasers	75
Shopkeepers	93	Vagrants	66
Lorry drivers	87	Demonstrators	55
Middle-class people	84	Juveniles	52
Working-class people	82	Long-haired hippy types	50
Delivery men	79	West Indians	42
Children under 14	78	Indians and Pakistanis	40

were most frequently rated as either very or fairly helpful and also the seven sub-groups which were most frequently rated as not particularly helpful or not at all helpful.

There were major differences in the ratings given to the different groups — though even for the predominantly unhelpful sub-groups of the population, there were substantial numbers of police officers who rated them helpful. Thus, 9 per cent rated skinheads and greasers as helpful; 17 per cent for vagrants; 25 per cent for long-haired hippy types; 35 per cent for Indians and Pakistanis; 36 per cent for West Indians; 36 per cent for juveniles. Furthermore, the balance of the ratings was decidedly on the 'helpful' half of the scale.

Police views about why different groups are helpful to the police

For the group ranked by a respondent as 'most helpful' in the list of twenty-three, the respondent was asked to say why he considered that group helpful. The reasons were content analysed and the salient features of that analysis were as follows:

1 Some of the reasons which were frequently volunteered for some single group were also dominant in this way for other groups, namely:

a. They rely on the police for help and protection; are helpful for reasons of self-interest (a major reason for: shopkeepers, old people, middle-class people, working-class people).
b. They appreciate or have respect for the job the police are doing (a major reason for: old people, middle-class people, lorry drivers, working-class people).

2 Other reasons given fairly frequently were:

a. They were brought up or taught to help and respect the police (e.g. old people, children under 14, upper-class people).
b. They have jobs or special characteristics or situations which enable them to be helpful to the police (e.g.

54

shopkeepers, lorry drivers, stall holders, taxi drivers, children under 14, working-class people).
c. They are honest, truthful, straightforward, law abiding, open (e.g. working-class people, children under 14, shopkeepers).

Police views about public helpfulness in different situations

Police respondents were asked to say how helpful they thought the public was with respect to twelve different situations (e.g. in answering questions for the police during an enquiry; reporting someone they believe is about to commit a crime). For each of these statements, the respondent rated the public on a scale; very helpful, fairly helpful, not particularly helpful, not helpful at all.

1 According to the police, the public's helpfulness varies markedly with the type of help concerned, being greatest (among the twelve types investigated) in relation to 'reporting something they've had stolen' and least for 'telling the police when they think someone is selling stolen goods'. Results for all twelve situations are set out in Table 23.

Table 23
Proportion of police saying the public is helpful in certain situations: police sample

Type of help	Proportion saying public is 'very' or 'fairly' helpful (%)	Type of help	Proportion saying public is 'very' or 'fairly' helpful (%)
Reporting something they've had stolen	96	Appearing in court as a witness in a police case	56
Answering questions for the police during an inquiry	86	Reporting someone they believe is about to commit a crime	55
Helping at the scene of an accident	71	Helping a policeman when he is in a dangerous situation	53
Telling children to look on the police as their friends	72	Reporting a motorist for driving dangerously	44
Reporting a disturbance in a house in their neighbourhood	67	Reporting someone they believe is in possession of drugs	42
Reporting vandalism to the police	66	Telling policemen when they think someone is selling stolen goods	37

2 Those situations with the lower ratings for helpfulness appear to involve all or some of the following elements: informing on someone else; informing on someone when it is not clear that this person is committing a crime; a situation where the respondent has nothing personal to gain or save.

3 On the basis of the evidence from the survey of adult opinions, it also appears that in general the public rates itself as more willing to give help to the police than the police believe is the case. The difference is especially marked with respect to: 'helping a policeman when he is in a dangerous situation'; 'reporting someone who is thought to be about to commit a crime'.

9 SUGGESTIONS OF POLICE OFFICERS FOR IMPROVING RELATIONS BETWEEN POLICE AND PUBLIC

Police officers were asked: to say what they thought should be done by the police to improve relations between police and public; for their views about the effectiveness of certain public relations work being done by the police; for their views about the ways in which the mass media present the police; for their views about mass media treatment of the police; for the names of the organizations which they think could do most to help police—public relations and of those which they feel have done most harm to them.

How could the Metropolitan Police Force improve relations between police and public?

Respondents were asked: 'What do you think the Metropolitan Police should do to improve their relations with the public?' Responses were subject to probing and to content analysis. The more recurrently volunteered suggestions were as follows:

1 'Increase the public's knowledge of the police, of their role, of their point of view, of the police job; increase the public's knowledge of the law' (325 references).

2 'Have more contact with the public when on duty' (317 references).

3 'Have more (home) beat officers, more police on cycles, fewer police in panda cars' (251 references).

4 'Improve relations through open days at or visits to police stations, make police stations more accessible, friendly' (216 references).

5 'Improve relations with the public through the mass media' (211 references).

6 'Improve relations through holding lectures, discussions, debates, talks, seminars' (195 references).

7 'Improve relations through (visits to) schools, through the education system' (191 references).

The more frequently-suggested agents of such changes were (apart from 'the police'), home beat officers, other beat officers, officers from specialist departments or branches of the Metropolitan Police Force.

The effectiveness of certain public realtions-type activities

Police officers rated each of a number of police-sponsored activities designed to be supportive of the police and their special roles (e.g. crime-prevention exhibitions, Police 5, the Juvenile Bureau scheme) in terms of their likely effect on police–public relations. These ratings are summarized in Table 24 below in very general terms.

Table 24

Proportion of police claiming good or bad effect

Police activity or service	Proportion claiming 'Good effect' (%)	'Bad effect' (%)
Talks and visits to schools and playgrounds	99	0
Police 5	98	—
Crime prevention exhibitions	94	—
Open days at police stations	93	—
Special projects to deal with specific problems, organized by Community Liaison Officers	85	1
Crime prevention leaflets	83	—
The Juvenile Bureau scheme	79	9
Advisory Clinics for special groups organized by Community Liaison Officers	78	3
Recruitment publicity and campaigns	61	1
Leaflets on rights when arrested	56	11
Leaflets on making a complaint against a police officer	45	25

The main indications of the data in this table are as follows:

1 There was a marked tendency for the police officer respondents to regard the activities specified to them as having a good effect on relations between police and public.

2 It is noteworthy that the distribution of leaflets concerning (a) making a complaint against a police officer and (b) rights when arrested . . . were, in spite of being bottom of the list in Table 24, endorsed as having a good effect by about half the respondents.

Table 25

Whether certain statements relating to the mass media presentation of the police are thought by police officers to be true or false

Views about mass media treatment of the police

Police respondents were asked to consider the truth or falsity of a number of statements about mass media

Statement considered by officers	Proportion of police officers		
	Saying 'true' (%)	Saying 'not true' (%)	N.I.* (%)
Newspapers: they are always too ready to show the police in a bad light	47	52	1
Television: they are always too ready to show the police in a bad light	19	81	—
Radio: they are always too ready to show the police in a bad light	11	83	6
Newspapers: When criticizing the police, they don't give the police enough opportunity to tell *their* side of the story	73	23	5
Television: When criticizing the police, they don't give the police enough opportunity to tell *their* side of the story	56	38	5
Radio: When criticizing the police, they don't give the police enough opportunity to tell *their* side of the story	54	35	11
When criticized by the media, the police don't take enough opportunity to tell their side of the story	86	12	2
Most television programmes dealing with the police show them as kind and understanding	56	43	2
Newspapers always publicize police acts of bravery	64	34	1
Most radio programmes on the police show them as intelligent, thinking people	57	33	10

*No information available

58

treatment of the police. The results are set out in Table 25 and their main indications are as follows.

1 The statement getting most frequent endorsement as 'true' was: 'when criticized by the media, the police don't take enough opportunity to tell their side of the story' (86 per cent endorsed this statement as true).

2 The Press is much more often rated as working against the good image of the police than are television or radio (in that order). This applies with respect both to (*a*) being too willing to show the police in a bad light and (*b*) not giving police officers enough opportunity to answer their critics.

3 Nonetheless, the respondents endorsed positive-sounding statements about each medium. Thus, the Press was seen by 64 per cent as always publicizing police acts of bravery; television by 56 per cent as showing the police to be kind and understanding; radio by 57 per cent as showing the police as 'intelligent, thinking people'.

Which organizations could do most to help relations between police and public and which do it most harm?

Police respondents considered sixteen organizations with a view to naming the top three in terms of the help they *could* give to police—public relations. Respondents were similarly asked to name three that had done most harm to police—public relations.

1 The organizations most frequently named as able to help were: youth clubs (29 per cent), education authorities (26 per cent), the Home Office (21 per cent), local community relations committees (18 per cent). On the other hand, certain organizations were rarely identified amongst the first three, namely: the Church, the Probation Service, social welfare agencies, National Union of Students.

2 Those most frequently named as doing most harm were: organizations dealing with citizens' rights (e.g. National Council for Civil Liberties) (50 per cent named them amongst the top three), immigrant associations (23 per

cent), National Union of Students (16 per cent), the courts (12 per cent).

10 KNOWLEDGEABILITY CONCERNING THE POLICE AND POLICING ARRANGEMENTS

Members of the adult sample and of the youth sample were questioned to determine how familiar they were with certain aspects of local and metropolitan policing arrangements.

Knowledgeability of adults and young people

Knowledgeability of adults

For the adult sample, the main indications of the responses to these questions were as follows.

1 Forty-five per cent could say where the nearest police station was and 10 per cent could name a local police officer.

2 Eighty-one per cent said that they had heard of the Special Constabulary and 61 per cent thought that there were 'specials' in the police force in London. Amongst the 81 per cent who had heard of the 'specials', there was a fairly high level of awareness of at least one of the ways in which the Special Constabulary differs from the regular force. A total of eighty-three persons (out of the 81 per cent who said they had heard of them) thought that they were special investigators of some kind, presumably indicating confusion with Special Branch. Twenty-eight persons thought they were trainee policemen.

3 Seventy-one per cent said they had never seen a crime prevention leaflet.

4 About a quarter of the adult sample claimed they see a uniformed police officer locally only occasionally (i.e. once a month or less or never) — though 31 per cent said they see one every day or more often. About half the London adults want to see policemen locally more often than they

do at present and practically all the rest were satisfied with present frequency of seeing them.

5 When asked what should be the principal mode of local patrol, 'car' and 'foot' were volunteered with equal frequency.

6 The great majority of opinions about traffic police were favourable and included explanations that the traffic police are essential, deter motorists from committing offences and help to prevent accidents, have a difficult job to do. Some respondents thought there were not enough of them. Adverse comments were principally that they are inefficient, drive too fast and set a bad example, are not strict enough with motoring offences, are sometimes petty in dealing with offences.

7 The great majority (88 per cent) thought it a good thing that the traffic wardens were taking over traffic duties formerly carried out by the police. Over the whole sample, 42 per cent thought that traffic wardens were doing their job very well, 49 per cent fairly well, and 6 per cent thought they were doing a poor job.

Knowledgeability of young people

Members of the youth sample were asked questions broadly similar to those asked of the adult sample. In addition they were asked if they had any personal experience with respect to the police activities referred to in Table 26 (all of these being of a kind designed to inform people about the police in order to develop better relations with them).

Table 26

Proportion of young people claiming personal experience of various P—R activities of the police

Types of public relations activity	Proportion saying 'yes' (%)
Looked at a leaflet or poster about the police	64
Been to a talk given by a policeman or policewoman	51
Had lessons or discussions at school about the police	38
Been to an exhibition or display about the police	38
Taken a cycling test arranged by the police	22
Taken part in a competition arranged by the police	9
Been to an open day at a police station	4
Been on an outing arranged by the police	2

1 The percentages who said 'yes' to the activities specified in Table 26 seem to provide clear pointers to the direction and character of future police work on the public relations front.

2 The respondents were also asked what they had learned from such contacts and experiences. The more recurrently-stated types of such learning were (in order of frequency of mention):

a. The nature of specific jobs that the police do, jobs they care about doing, how and why they do them, what equipment they use.
b. How the public can help with road safety.
c. Recruitment information, standards required for entry into the force, joining procedure, careers information.
d. How the police can help the public.
e. Information about conditions of employment and about the job of being a police officer.
f. Favourable comments about working conditions.
g. How the public can help the police.
h. How the public can help the police in crime prevention.

3 In a further questioning sequence, respondents were asked about what personal acquaintance they had with the police officers, their knowledge of their local police and of local policing arrangements, what they knew of the Juvenile Bureau and of related matters, and so on. The principal indications of their responses were as follows:

a. Thirty-three per cent of the young-person sample said that they knew a police officer personally, with about half of these saying they saw this officer more frequently than once a month.
b. About half the respondents knew where their local police station was, and about one in eight could name a local police officer.
c. Twenty-three per cent said they had heard of the Juvenile Bureau and 4 per cent that they had been cautioned by the Juvenile Bureau. When questioned about what the Juvenile Bureau was and did, there was hardly an adequate reply, most of the respondents either confusing the Juvenile Bureau with some other body or failing to mention its special connection with the police.

d. Respondents were asked if they had ever thought of becoming a police officer and what they thought of the idea of so doing. About a quarter said that they *had* at some time thought of becoming a police officer and the tendency to say this was slightly greater among those who knew a police officer personally.

The expressed views about becoming a police officer were more often negative than positive. The principal positive comments were: (*a*) concerned with pay, promotion, stability, hours of work, duties, sporting activities; (*b*) that the job of police officer was worth while, important, necessary; (*c*) that the police are respected and trusted. The principal negative comments were: (*a*) concerned with working conditions (i.e. pay, promotion, hours of work, duties); (*b*) that the respondent would not like the duties involved; (*c*) that the respondent would not like to have to wear the police uniform; (*d*) that the respondent did not like the public's attitude towards the police, would lose friends, would become unpopular.

Some facts about police officers

In this same general context, *police officers* were questioned about themselves, (e.g. about place of residence, educational background, number of complaints (if any) made against them, reading behaviour, community involvement). Some of the more salient results were as follows:

1 Thirty-one per cent of officers live in police communities and 69 per cent in the general community.

2 The age of finishing full-time education is higher for police than for the general public.

3 Compared with the general population, the fathers of police officers are drawn slightly less from the ABC1* classes, much more from the C2* classes and much less from the DE* classes.

*These are the socio-economic gradings used by the Joint Industry Committee for National Readership Surveys: ABC1 = the upper-middle, the middle and the lower-middle classes; C2 = the skilled working class; DE = other working classes and 'those at the lower levels of subsistence'.

4 About a quarter of the force had been in the armed forces just prior to joining the Metropolitan Police Force and about half had been in the armed forces at some time. Nearly a quarter had been in a cadet corps or in an officer training corps while at school.

5 Some 58 per cent said that there had been at least one complaint registered against them, though the great majority claimed that such complaint(s) had been dismissed. In the view of police officers, the more frequently-named 'things' complained about (i.e. by complainants) were: police abruptness, sarcasm, officiousness, brutality, assault, use of force; wrongful, unlawful or unjust arrest; persecution; insufficient care for the interests of the public; police inactivity. The more frequently-named classes of complainant were: criminals, offenders, prisoners; people on the criminal verge; people with something to hide; motorists; coloured people, coloured immigrants; upper- or upper-middle-class; middle-class people.

6 Some 13 per cent said they were thinking of leaving the Metropolitan Police Force before normal retirement. Reasons given for this were principally: financial reasons; because the police officer wants a better job or to better himself; because of shift work involved in police duties; because he is dissatisfied with the promotion system or worried about career prospects; because he wants to run his own business; because he doesn't like the job or is not suited to it. *Only very few mentioned a reason connected with police–public relations.*

7 About one in six of the officers interviewed said they helped in the community in some way in their off-duty time. About one in four claimed that three-quarters or more of their friends were police officers and somewhat more than that claimed that three-quarters or more of their friends were *non-police.*

8 Daily newspapers read regularly by police officers were principally: the *Daily Express* (45 per cent claim they read this regularly), the *Evening News* (42 per cent), *Daily Telegraph* (34 per cent), *Daily Mirror* (26 per cent). These levels of readership are sharply out of line with the levels for the general public, namely 22, 31, 13 and 34 per cent respectively. Sunday newspaper reading by police officers is similarly out of step with Sunday newspaper reading by the public. The police and the public figures for *Sunday Express, Sunday Mirror, Sunday Telegraph, The People, News of the World* are respectively: 57, 28, 23, 22, 21 per cent and 27, 32, 7, 30 and 33 per cent. The great majority of the police say they look at a local newspaper 'nowadays'.

11 COMPARING ATTITUDES AND BEHAVIOUR IN DIFFERENT POPULATION SECTORS

The information gathered was analysed by certain of the characteristics of the respondents. For both the adult and the young-person samples, these characteristics were: age, sex, skin colour, social class or grade, area of residence, whether a motorist. For the police sample, the characteristics in terms of which the analysis was made were: class of duty, rank, place of work, length of service, physical build, number of complaints registered against the respondent, proportion of friends who are police officers, miles driven per week on duty, miles per week off duty.

Variations for members of the public

By age

Within the context of overall approval of the police, there is a pattern of variation by age of respondent. Thus, approval is at its greatest amongst those aged 65 years and over, is somewhat less for the 51—64 years group, less again for those aged 41—50, and so on to its lowest level amongst the 18—20-year olds. Thereafter, the level of approval tends to increase through to the 13—14-year olds — though not to anything like the high level of the 65 and over group. At the same time, there are some aspects of reaction to the police that vary but little with the ages of the respondents.

By sex

For adult Londoners, there is an overall tendency for women to be more supportive of the police than are men and this tendency is fairly common over the wide range of attitudes studied. Within the youth sample (13 to 20 years), the same overall tendency was operative, with girls being more favourably disposed than boys. At the same time, girls had less contact with police officers and were little different from boys in their views about whether the police had too much power.

By skin colour

Coloured people, irrespective of age, were less satisfied than white people with the London police — though in the adult sample at least, coloured people exhibited a greater supportiveness for the police *function* than did the whites. The small size of the coloured sub-samples does, however, call for wariness in generalizing from these findings.

By area of residence

For both adults and young people, there is in general relatively little difference in attitudes between those living in the inner and the outer parts of London.

By social class

For adult Londoners, the evidence suggests that those in the *lower* social grades place *more* importance upon the police doing their various jobs and tend somewhat more than others to regard the police as doing those jobs well. On the other hand, they tend to be somewhat *less* willing to be helpful to the police. Broadly the same results apply for the youth sample — though in addition, the lower social grades tend less to trust the police and somewhat more to be afraid of them. For both samples, there are many aspects of attitude towards the police for which social class is not discriminating.

By motoring background

Adult motorists, especially those who do a lot of driving, are in general less favourably disposed towards the police than are adults who are non-motorists. Within the *youth* sample, non-motorists tend to like the police more than motorists, to think more highly of them in terms of their characteristics and to appreciate more the way they do their job. But they differ little from motorists in terms of willingness to help the police, and in their views about police having too much power.

Variations in outlook amongst police officers

Throughout the full report on police attitudes towards the public, the results were analysed by each of the eleven variables listed in the introduction to this section. In general, there was relatively little evidence of big differences or of consistent trends in going from one sub-group of the police force to another.

Main Findings

What follows is a list of salient findings amongst those reported on pp. 6 to 67 of this extended summary of three major reports.

1 a. In terms of being broadly satisifed with the police, liking, trusting and respecting them, the judgments of adult Londoners tend to be markedly favourable. Similarly, there was a marked tendency for adults to rate the police highly in terms of personal characteristics and abilities such as well trained, calm, efficient, courteous, fair, kind, intelligent, friendly.
b. The reactions and judgments of young people (aged 13 to 20 years) were also, in general, quite favourable, but less so than those of the adult public.
c. The police themselves, though correctly judging the public's reactions to be favourable, quite appreciably underestimate the *degree* to which those reactions are favourable.

2 Despite the overall favourableness of the public's reactions to the police, and evidence of sympathetic insight into the special difficulties of the police, many criticisms of them are made in relation to specific matters. Some of these criticisms come from relatively small percentages of the population but nonetheless involve many people. At the personal level the criticisms relate to behaviour such as rudeness and bad temper, bullying, allowing one's mood to determine the action taken, using too much force in certain situations, unfairness in dealing with some kinds of people, failing to show gratitude when help is given or discouraging help when it is offered, dishonesty in some police officers. There were also criticisms directed at police practice generally (e.g. the use of unfair methods for getting information, hushing-up complaints against the police, beating-up people held in police stations, abuse of police powers, police forcing their way into homes, the unavailability of a policeman when wanted, preventing arrested people getting in touch with a solicitor soon enough).

3 The great majority of those who endorse adverse views of police practices say that they have not come across such practices personally but have formed their impressions principally on the basis of newspaper and television content and of hearsay.

4 Members of the public, especially young people, are in general poorly informed about many aspects of the work of the police. This applies particularly to local policing arrangements and to the nature of the powers of the police. In addition, a great many people have as yet not been reached by police services designed to inform people and to develop constructive contact with them.

5 Public ratings of the importance of different police duties tend to be out of line with judgments about how well these duties are carried out. For example, adult Londoners rated 'catching professional criminals' as the most important police job but graded it eighth in a list of eighteen duties in terms of how well it was done; young people graded 'catching people who take drugs' as third (out of fourteen) in terms of its importance as a police task, but tenth in terms of how well it was done.

6 The proportion of the public who would contact the police in various circumstances, varies quite markedly with the situation. Amongst adults, for example, practically all would contact the police if their home was burgled but only a third if they knew someone was selling stolen property. Willingness to contact the police was lower for young people than for adults. A wide range of reasons for 'doing nothing' was offered.

7 The great majority of adults and young people claimed that, given a chance they would in general help the police, and about half the sampled population rated themselves as *very* helpfully disposed. However, just as with willingness to

contact the police, willingness to help varied with the circumstances. Thus, for adults, it was higher for things like telling children to look on the police as their friends, answering questions for the police during an enquiry helping at the scene of an accident, and lower for things like reporting a motorist who goes through a red light, appearing in court as a witness in a police case. Circumstances named as working against being helpful are given separately for adults and young people. These include: the likelihood of trouble or retaliation for the person giving the help, the lack of confidentiality about help given, not knowing enough about how to help the police, embarrassment over what 'the neighbours' would think, a belief that offenders get off too lightly, a belief that the police don't really want help, a view that the police are not very helpful themselves.

8 Police officers bring to bear on their work a social outlook which varies substantially from officer to officer but which tends generally to be featured by both non-cynicism and strictness. With exceptions, they tend to regard the public generally as being at least fairly honest, reliable, friendly and kind towards each other; as fairly non-violent; as fairly selfish and apathetic; as somewhat suspicious of each other. With regard to their view of different groups and minorities in society, there is a general tendency towards strictness and conservatism of outlook, though this outlook appears to be tempered by a substantial degree of reality and of humanitarianism.

9 Police officers had much to say about ways of improving relations between themselves and the public. Some of the more recurrently offered suggestions were: increase the public's knowledge of the police and their roles; increase contact with the public on and off duty both informally and through such arrangements as open days at police stations, public lectures and debates, school visits; have more officers walking a beat; step up present public relations work by the police. With respect to mass media presentation of the police, there was major endorsement of the view that the police 'don't take enough opportunity to tell their side of the story when criticized'.

Recommendations

The position presented in the reports on the adult and the youth surveys is that, whereas the public is in general favourably disposed towards the Metropolitan Police Force, many criticisms of the Force are made in relation to specific matters. The generally favourable view held by the public rests upon approval of many aspects of police behaviour and a degree of sympathetic insight into the special difficulties of the policing role. This combination at present appears to cushion the general image of the police against the many specific criticisms that are made, but it cannot be assumed that this will continue to be so. Indeed it would be unwise to discount the possibility that the present level of criticism is the beginning of a trend. In any case, the present level and nature of criticism seems to call for remedial action of a concentrated kind and it is to this end that the following recommendations are made.

CONCERNING THE DISTRIBUTION OF THIS REPORT

It is recommended that this summary report be brought in its entirety to the attention of police officers generally in the Metropolitan Police Force so that they may become more fully aware of how the public perceives them and feels about them. The case for so doing is as follows.

1 The police at present underestimate the general favourableness of the public's attitude towards them and the public's willingness to be helpful.

2 Notwithstanding the generally favourable attitude of the public, there are in the public's view of the police substantial elements of criticism, of disquiet and of

misunderstanding that police officers themselves would benefit by knowing about. It is important, too, that police officers be made aware of the inquiry's finding that the level of criticism and of misunderstanding amongst young people is greater than amongst adults.

It is particularly important that the report should go to those with a special responsibility for training recruits to the Force.

CONCERNING THE MODIFICATION OF CERTAIN FORMS OF BEHAVIOUR BY INDIVIDUAL POLICE OFFICERS

Steps should be taken to reduce as much as possible the incidence of any unnecessary aspects of police behaviour which irritate or annoy people and serve generally to reduce goodwill and co-operation between the police and the public.

Certain of the public's criticisms relate to the personal behaviour of officers, the more recurrent of the criticisms being: rudeness and bad temper, bullying, allowing one's mood to determine the action taken, using too much force in certain situations, unfairness in dealing with some kinds of people, failing to show gratitude when help is given or discouraging help when it is offered. Whether views such as these be well founded or not, they are the views that many people hold about the behaviour of some police officers. Special attention should therefore be given to modifying, wherever possible and desirable, those aspects of police outlook and behaviour that give support to such views.

The methods suitable for achieving such ends will need to be geared to police functioning and facilities but they should include measures of the following kinds:

1 Intensified instruction at the training establishments of the Metropolitan Police Force.

2 Specialized programmes of instruction for mature officers, possibly including discussion sessions between members of the public and police officers.

Appropriately-presented information drawn from this summary report, or from the full report, might well form a useful background for such training or re-training.

CONCERNING AN EXAMINATION OF CERTAIN OPERATIONAL PRACTICES OF THE POLICE

Some of the criticisms made of the police go beyond the behaviour of the individual police officer, being offered more as criticisms of police practice. These criticisms include: unfair methods of getting information; hushing-up complaints against the police; beating-up of people held in police stations; abuse of police powers; police forcing their way into homes; the unavailability of a policeman when wanted; preventing arrested people getting in touch with a solicitor soon enough. Whether true or not, these views exist in an appreciable number of people and this calls initially for an examination by the police of their own operating practices. To the extent that the claims are untrue, corrective publicity by the police will be called for.

PROVIDING THE PUBLIC WITH INFORMATION ABOUT THE POLICE

Steps additional to what is being done already should be taken in order to inform the public more thoroughly about relevant aspects of the duties, the methods and the achievements of the police. The evidence from the three inquiries suggests that in extending such a service, special attention should be given to providing information on the following topics.

1 The role of the police as keepers of law and order, as distinct from law *makers*.

2 What the duties of the police are (and are not) and why certain socially abrasive jobs have to be done by them (e.g. stopping people in the street to search them).

3 The powers of the police — both their extent and their limitations.

4 Police methods of investigating complaints made against members of the Force.

73

5 The rights of individuals within aspects of the law especially relevant to police—public relations.

6 The different ways in which the public can help the police and the degree to which the police need their help.

7 Why it is sensible to contact the police in certain situations.

8 How to get information about one's local police service.

9 What it is like to be a police officer.

10 Police-thinking about motorized and foot patrols and the special role of the man on the beat.

11 The special achievements of the Metropolitan Police Force and of those who serve in it.

The manner of imparting such information will have to be linked to the varying backgrounds and ages of the intended recipients and this will call for the application of specialized knowledge of communication experts both within and beyond the Force. Presumably, such information would be imparted through the mass media and through various activities organized by the police themselves. Indeed, there is widespread support amongst police officers for special police operations in the form of: talks and visits to schools and playgrounds; extension of the 'Police 5' type of broadcast; crime-prevention exhibitions; open days at police stations; special projects to deal with specific problems, organized by Community Liaison officers; crime-prevention leaflets; the Juvenile Bureau scheme; advisory clinics for special groups, organized by Community Liaison officers.

The individual policeman on his beat is also in a position to play an important part in this communication process. This is principally because he is well placed for making personal and friendly contact with people and in this special situation can effectively pass out information when requested or volunteer it on relevent matters.

The position of young people calls especially for attention in that young people are less informed about the police than are adults. Thus, there are very many young people who have: never been to a police exhibition or display; never taken a cycling test arranged by the police; never been to an open day at a police station; never been to a talk given by a police officer; never had a lesson or discussion at school about the police. In view of this, there seems to be a case for an extension or an intensification of police-organized activities of the kinds listed above, designed to inform young people on matters relating to the police and the jobs they do.

In this particular context, it may be well to consider (a) how far and on what scale the direct teaching of children about the police and their functions can be taken within the school curriculum — or indeed within pre-school programmes; (b) the nature of the films, slides and other aids that might be prepared for informing the young within or outside of the school system; (c) the degree to which the various media (and especially schools broadcasting services and children's broadcasting) can be further utilized for the presentation of such information, no doubt in the context of some broader coverage of the social services; (d) the degree to which police officers themselves should participate in such activities.

In intensifying or extending an information service in the recommended ways, it is most important that it be operated and maintained solely to provide information and that special care be taken to prevent its use as a propaganda instrument.

INCREASING PERSONAL CONTACT BETWEEN THE POLICE AND THE PUBLIC

One strong indication of the findings was that personal contact of the public with police officers was important in maintaining a co-operative relationship. Certainly it is much easier for hearsay and unfounded charges in the mass media to take hold of people in the absence of any personal contact with 'real-life' police officers. The methods of ensuring such contact are best considered within the operational framework of the Force, but a policeman walking his community beat is clearly a very important element in any such operation.

75

In this respect it is particularly important to be aware that the majority of the young people questioned did not know any police officer personally. Along with this there is a strong tendency for young people to reach decisions about the character and the behaviour of the police in the absence of direct experience.

The development of a greater degree of personal contact between police officers and the public would of course call for a favourable attitude towards this on the part of police officers. In fact, the evidence of this inquiry indicates that for the majority of officers this requirement is largely met. Thus, there is amongst them a large degree of support for such things as: living *within* the general community; increasing the public's knowledge about the police, about police jobs and about the law; having more home beat officers and generally increasing the extent to which officers walk a beat rather than driving around in cars; the greater use of open days at police stations; the holding of courses, discussion groups, debates and talks in which members of the public take part.

The development of a fuller and more useful degree of contact between police and public would be facilitated by a greater willingness or ability, on the part of police officers, to smile in appropriate situations!

CONCERNING THE ATTITUDES OF COLOURED PEOPLE

The evidence suggests that there is a fairly consistent tendency for coloured people to be less favourably disposed towards the police than are white people. However, the number of coloured persons in the sample was, as must be expected on a proportionate basis, relatively small — so that the reported findings can be regarded as no more than general pointers to the real situation. It is highly desirable that a further survey be conducted with viable numbers of both coloured and white persons to check the important indications of the present inquiry.

CONCERNING RECRUITMENT TO THE FORCE

Certain of the evidence in this report raises important considerations for those responsible for recruitment policy and for its implementation. This evidence relates particularly to the criticism levelled by some sections of the public at police officers, as reported in this document (e.g. in terms of rudeness, bad temper, bullying, failure to show gratitude when helped, unfairness to some kinds of people, dishonesty to some degree).

Accepting that criticism may in some or many cases be ungrounded, it is nonetheless highly desirable that recruitment processes should, amongst their other purposes, be sharpened to eliminate selection of persons whose personality and character are likely to be unnecessarily abrasive with regard to public relations.

The findings with regard to the social philosophy of the police are also of relevance to recruitment policy and should be closely examined in the context of the efficient functioning of the Force.

EVALUATING THE STEPS TAKEN

It is desirable that periodic checks be made on the effectiveness of the actions taken to further co-operation between the police and the public, whether that action takes the form of exhibitions, a film on general release, slides shown at schools, a radio or television series or service, a programme of one-day visits to police stations. Relatively inexpensive research procedures are available for doing such work and can provide an early indication of how successful or otherwise is the communication effort concerned.

TAKING NOTE OF THE VIEWS OF POLICE OFFICERS IN THE GENERAL CONTEXT OF PUBLIC RELATIONS AND LAW ENFORCEMENT

Certain of the findings about the views of police officers have special relevance for management and policy in the area of police—public relations and it is strongly recommended that these views be carefully studied in that context. Whereas some of these views have already been referred to in relation to other of the recommendations, it is desirable that they be presented here as a whole even if this involves some degree of repetition. Thus, special note should be taken of the following:

1 the experience of police officers that certain groups within the public have tended more than others to create problems and work for the police;

2 the widely-endorsed views of officers that wherever possible police officers should live within the general community and that police officers should have opportunity to take part in community activities in their on-duty hours; that public relations would be improved by having more officers walk a beat;

3 the widespread support of police officers for special police operations in the form of talks and visits to schools and playgrounds, Police 5, crime-prevention exhibitions, open days at police stations, special projects to deal with specific problems organized by community liaison officers, crime-prevention leaflets, the Juvenile Bureau scheme, advisory clinics for special groups organized by community liaison officers;

4 the widespread views of police officers (a) that, 'when criticized by the media, the police don't take enough opportunity to tell their side of the story', (b) that the Press more often works against the good image of the police than do the other media, (c) that there are certain kinds of things done by the Press and the other media that are constructive to the police image;

5 the widespread view of police officers that the police view should be presented more forcefully in an attempt to change laws that are unfair or unenforceable;

6 the fact that 30 per cent endorse, and about 60 per cent reject, the view that 'complaints against police officers should be investigated by suitably qualified people outside the police force';

78

7 the fact that there is an overall tendency for police officers to agree that police powers are about right as they are, but that nonetheless there are exceptions to this at the individual level and in terms of certain situations (especially enforcing obscenity laws, dealing with juveniles who break the law, enforcing the payment of fines).

Consideration should also be given to the suggestions of police officers concerning ways in which the relations between police and public might be bettered. These are detailed in the full report but those that were more frequently volunteered are as follows:

1 Increase the public's knowledge of the police, of the police role, of the police point of view, of the police job; increase the public's knowledge of the law.

2 See that the police get more contact with the public when on duty.

3 Have more home beat/beat officers, more police on bicycles, fewer police in panda cars.

4 Improve relations with the public through open days at, or visits to, police stations; make stations more accessible, friendly.

5 Improve relations with the public through the mass media.

6 Improve relations through holding courses, discussions, debates, talks, seminars.

7 Improve relations through visits to schools, through the education system.

Appendices I & II

Presenting in Condensed Form the Questionnaires used in the Adult and the Police Surveys

The two questionnaires presented here are 'condensed' in the sense that there is no representation of the *space* for answers and coding that was laid out in them when used in their respective surveys. This has meant a space saving in the present document. At the same time, the reader will find in the condensed statement a faithful representation of the questions and of the eliciting procedures used. Access to questionnaires in their full working form is available through the Metropolitan Police to qualified persons. The questionnaire used in the youth survey was closely similar to that used in the adult survey and this is available in full through the same source.

In the interests of simplicity of presentation, the terms 'he' or 'his' have been used throughout (instead of he/she and his/hers) in referring to the respondent and to the interviewer. It may be taken however that in each survey the sample was made up, in representative proportions, of male and female respondents and that the interviewing team working on the survey included both men and women.

Also for brevity and simplicity of presentation, there is little reference in the condensed questionnaires to the *order* of presentation of statements and of the response systems from which respondents could choose replies. These were all subject to systematic rotation through the use of different visual aid packs.

The extended summary of the full report, as presented in this document, does of necessity deal only briefly with the other aspects of research methodology employed in the investigation. Here, too, extensive detail is presented in the full report.

Appendix I
A condensed form of the
Adult Questionnaire

INTRODUCTION AND PREPARATORY QUESTIONING

In this introductory section of the questionnaire, the interviewer briefly introduced himself and the enquiry. He then asked a short series of questions designed to identify, and then to screen out, persons who did not qualify for interview, namely: those who had lived in the Metropolitan Police District for less than six months; those who normally live in London for less than six months a year; those who are full time members of the regular police force.

SECTION I: Concerning the respondent's more general feelings with regard to the Metropolitan Police.

In this section of the questionnaire, the respondent used rating scales to indicate the degree to which he was SATISFIED with the London Police, the degree to which he RESPECTED them, the degree to which he LIKED them, the degree to which he TRUSTED them, the degree to which he felt AT EASE with them.

The questioning procedure took the following form.

Q.1 "As I said, we're interested in finding out how people feel about the London Police." (*If Respondent lives in an outer area, he is told*: "You probably know that this area comes under the London police.") "How do you feel about the London police?" *This question is not probed. It is asked solely to bring 'forward in the respondent's mind' his normally available thoughts about the London Police.*

Q.2 "Now I am going to hand you some cards. For each one, I want you to pick the statement which is the *closest* to the way you feel, in general, about the London police." *The Respondent is shown a card listing the following possible answers*: I DO NOT FEEL AT ALL SATISFIED WITH THEM/ I DO NOT FEEL VERY SATISFIED WITH THEM/ I FEEL FAIRLY SATISFIED WITH THEM/ I FEEL VERY SATISFIED WITH THEM. *His choice is coded on the questionnaire. The order of these possible answers is reversed for one half of the sample.*
 The respondent is now told: "The rest are done in just the same way" *and he is taken progressively through four more rating operations dealing respectively with* : RESPECT FOR THE POLICE/ LIKING FOR THE POLICE/ TRUST OF THE POLICE/ FEELING AT EASE WITH THE POLICE.

SECTION 2: Concerning the respondent's views about how well the police do certain jobs and about which jobs they should be doing.

In this section of the questionnaire, the respondent was asked to consider a range of specific jobs 'that the police might do' and to rate each in terms of how well the police did them. There were eighteen of these jobs namely: preventing crime . . . talking to children who won't go to school . . . catching people who steal things that aren't worth much . . . catching professional criminals . . . dealing with parking offences . . . stopping a play or a film that may be immoral . . . dealing with children who break the law . . . controlling crowds at demonstrations . . . controlling crowds at football matches . . . catching motorists who have been drinking . . . helping to run things like youth clubs . . . catching people who take drugs . . . helping people who are lost, stranded or ill . . . getting back stolen property . . . helping to settle family rows . . . directing traffic . . . advising motorists about their driving . . . protecting people who have been threatened by someone. With respect to each of these jobs, the respondent chose a rating from the following set of answers: VERY WELL/ FAIRLY WELL/ NOT VERY WELL/ BADLY. Following this, the respondent rated the same jobs in terms of how important he considered them to be as jobs for the *police* to do. *The rating scale in this case was*: VERY IMPORTANT/ FAIRLY IMPORTANT/ NOT VERY IMPORTANT/ NOT AT ALL IMPORTANT/ NOT A JOB FOR THEM AT ALL. Where a job was rated as not one for the police, the respondent was asked to explain *why* he said that and to say who, then, should it be done by.

The questioning procedure took the following form.

Q.1 "Now I'm going to go through various jobs that the police *might do*. Here is the first of them: (*The interviewer now calls out the first in his list*, e.g., 'preventing crime'). *The interviewer pauses and then says slowly*: "From what you know of the London police, how well do you think they do the job of — — — — (*The interviewer repeats that job*)". *The respondent is shown the choice of reply card and is asked* : "Which of the answers on this card comes closest to your opinion about how well they do the job of — — — —?" *The rest of the jobs are dealt with in the same way and are progressively coded on the questionnaire.*

Q.2 "Now I want to go through these jobs again. But this time the question is different. Let's take the first job — — — — (*The interviewer reads it out*). In your opinion how important is it for the London police to do the job of — — — — (*The interviewer names the job*)?" *The respondent is shown the choice of reply card and is asked*: "Which of the answers on this card comes closest to your views about how important it is for the London police to do the job of — — — —. Read them all aloud please then choose the one that is closest to how *you* feel." *The rest of the jobs are dealt with in the same way.*

83

Q.3 "You say that — — — — (*The interviewer reads out job name*) was not a job for the London police at all. Why do you say that?" *The question is subject to probing.*

Q.4 *For each job designated by respondent as not one for the police at all, the interviewer asks*: "Who, then, should do the job of — — — — (*interviewer reads out job name*)."

SECTION 3: Concerning the respondent's views about the characteristics of the police.

In this section of the questionnaire, the respondent is asked to rate the police in terms of fifteen different characteristics, namely: *friendly, rude, courteous, *frightening, kind, *interfering, fair, calm, *bullying, efficient, dishonest, intelligent, *distant, *secretive, well-trained. For each characteristic, the rating scale was in the form: EXTREMELY/ VERY/ FAIRLY/ JUST A BIT/ NOT AT ALL. For certain of the characteristics (the ones marked with an asterisk), the respondent was asked if he thought it a good or a bad thing that the police were as he had just claimed. The questioning procedure used was as follows:

Q.1 "Now I shall read out some of the things people have said the police are like. I want you to tell me which ones describe what *you* think the police are like. Let's take the first: — — — — (*the interviewer now calls out the first characteristic, , e.g. 'friendly'*) Do you think that the police are in general — — — —?"
The response to this open-ended question, which is purely for 'warming up' purposes, is not coded. Whatever the reply given, the interviewer next asks: "So how — — — — (*the characteristic is repeated*) would you say the police are in general? Choose your answer from this card" *The choice is made from a card presenting the rating scale described above. This rating task is repeated for each characteristic against the same scale, the latter being kept continuously in front of the respondent. Responses are progressively coded.*

Q.2 *For each of the characteristics with an asterisk in front of it (see above)*, Question 2 is asked: "Do you think it is a good thing or a bad thing that the police are — — — —?" (*Here the interviewer reads back both the characteristic and the respondent's rating*).

SECTION 4: Concerning the respondent's impressions about how the police treat certain minority groups.

In this section of the questionnaire, the sub-groups and minorities asked about were: motorists, 'long haired hippie types', teenagers and young people, demonstrators, coloured people, Irish people, poor people, rich people and, for contrast, the general public. With

84

respect to each of these the respondent was asked if he thinks the police do certain things, namely: PUSH THEM AROUND/ LET THEM GET AWAY WITH THINGS/ TREAT THEM THE SAME AS ANYONE ELSE/ PICK ON THEM/ ARE ESPECIALLY HELPFUL TO THEM/ ARE QUICKER TO ARREST THEM. The questioning procedure used was as follows.

Q.1 "I'm going to give you a booklet. On each page is a different group of people. The first is — — — — (*the interviewer calls out the name of one of the groups*, e.g., 'motorists'). "Here are some of the ways in which the London police might treat — — — —(*The interviewer again names the group and points to a list of 'ways'* e.g., 'push them around'). Do you think it is *true* or *not true* that the London police — — — — (*the interviewer links the name of the group and the specified form of the treatment*, e.g., 'push motorists around'?) "*The respondent is led to deal in this manner with the other 'ways' for the group concerned and then deals with the next group in the same manner.*

Q.2 *After delivering Question 1 about a specific group, the interviewer asks question 2 with respect to each of the 'ways' that have been endorsed by the respondent as 'true'.* "You say that the police — — — —. Do you think this is a good thing or a bad thing?"

Responses to questions 1 and 2 are entered on the coding grids attached to the Questionnaire.

SECTION 5: Concerning the situations in which the respondent would or would not contact the police.

In this section of the questionnaire the respondent is asked, for each of a number of situations, if he *would* get in touch with the police, *might* get in touch with the police, *would not* get in touch with the police. The situations were as follows: If you lost your purse or wallet . . . If your house was burgled . . . If a child of yours was lost . . . If you knew someone was selling something that had been pinched . . . If you knew someone had a gun that he hadn't got a licence for . . . If you saw a stranger hanging around for a long time in your street . . . If a stranger made an indecent suggestion to you . . . If you saw some teenagers damaging a telephone kiosk . . . If you knew one of your neighbours was driving a stolen car . . . If you saw a fight in a cafe . . . If you were the only person to see a car accident. The questioning procedure used was as follows.

Q.1 "I'll read out some occasions when you might or might not *get in touch* with the police. By 'getting in touch' I mean telephoning or writing to them, talking to them in the street or going to the police station. (*Pause*) I'd like you to tell me whether you think you *would* or *would not* get in touch with them. Choose your answer from this card." *The card shown has on it the choice of answers*: I WOULD GET IN TOUCH WITH THE POLICE/ I MIGHT GET IN TOUCH WITH THE POLICE/ I WOULD NOT GET IN TOUCH WITH THE POLICE. *The respondent is asked to read out all three, after which the interviewer says*: "The first of these situations is — — — — (*the interviewer reads out the first situation on his list*, e.g., 'if you lost

85

your purse or wallet'). What would you do if − − − − (*the situation is repeated*)?" *The rest of the situations are dealt with in the same way.*

Q.2 *For each situation where the respondent* WOULD NOT *get in touch with the police the interviewer says:* "You said you would not get in touch with the police if − − − −. Why is that?" *Probing methods are used to get a full reply.*

SECTION 6: Concerning the respondent's views about how the police behave in various situations.

In this section of the questionnaire, the respondent is asked to express his opinion about how policemen behave in each of the following situations: at the scene of a road accident . . . at a home that has been burgled . . . at a demonstration . . . when bringing bad news . . . when stopping a motorist for an offence . . . when stopping someone in the street to search him . . . when giving someone directions . . . at the police station when someone comes to ask them something . . . when dealing with children who have done something wrong . . . on the telephone when someone phones them up to report something. With respect to each of these situations, the respondent was asked to endorse or reject a number of descriptions of behaviour, these being varied to fit the different situations. Thus for 'at the scene of a road accident' the descriptions on offer were: 'police are courteous' . . . 'police are rude' . . . 'police are efficient' . . . 'police are unkind' . . . 'police push people around' . . . 'police are flustered' . . . 'police are inefficient' . . . 'police are kind' . . . 'police are calm'. A booklet was used for this information gathering process, with one page per situation. The questioning procedure was as follows.

Q.1 "I am going to read out a number of situations and I would like you to tell me how you think the police behave in these situations. Here is the first: − − − −." *The interviewer reads out the first situation,* e.g., 'at the scene of an accident', *and passes over the booklet itself, saying:* "Here are a number of ways in which the police might behave − − − − (*naming the situation*). Would you please look at them." *After a pause, the interviewer continues with:* "Look at the words in each of these spaces. If the word in the space describes how the police behave − − − − (*the interviewer again names the situation*), put a cross in that space. If the words in that space *don't* describe how the police behave − − − − (*the interviewer again names the situation*) , put a cross in that space. The first word is − − − − (*the interviewer reads it out, e.g., 'courteous'*). Do you think the police, in general are − − − − in the way they behave − − − − (*the interviewer again reads out the situation*). *The respondent marks the square with a tick or a cross or 'don't know'. He deals with each of the descriptive terms. He then moves on to the next situation and does the same with that.*

Q.2 *At the end of this process, the interviewer asks about the respondent's personal experience of the police in the situations asked about:* "Now I want to ask you a few more questions about these situations. Would you please look at this card." *On the card are listed the various situations already asked about. The interviewer says:* "Here is the first situation (*he names the first on the list*)." "Have you ever had personal experience of the police in this situation? By personal experience I mean *being involved with it* or *seeing it happen.*" *This process is continued for all the other listed situations.*

SECTION 7: Concerning the respondent's position with regard to helping the police.

In this section of the questionnaire, the respondent is first asked to say how helpful, generally speaking, he would be to the London police, to explain the answer given, and to say what he thinks might be done to get people to be more helpful. After this, the interviewer takes the respondent through each of eleven different ways of helping the police, asking of each if the respondent has ever done that and how willing or otherwise he would be to do that in the future. The eleven 'ways' asked about were as follows: reporting something you've had stolen . . . answering questions for the police during an enquiry . . . helping at the scene of an accident . . . reporting a disturbance at a house nearby . . . helping a policeman when he's in a dangerous situation . . . reporting a disturbance in the street . . . asking the police to keep an eye on your home when you are away . . . telling children to look on the police as their friends . . . reporting a motorist for going through a red traffic light . . . reporting someone you believe is about to commit a crime . . . appearing in court as a witness in a police case. For each of the situations in which the respondent would *not* be willing to help the police in the future, he is asked to explain why and the question is subject to probing.

Later in this section, respondents who are less than willing to appear in court 'as a police witness' are asked to react to a series of statements presenting reasons for not wanting to give evidence in court. Finally, all respondents are asked to judge the truth or falsity, as they see the matter, of a series of seventeen statements bearing on giving help to the police, namely: the police get fed up with people who come to them over trivial things . . . when you report something to the police, you have to give your name even if you don't want to . . . a lot of crimes aren't likely to be solved, so it's not much use telling the police about them . . . if you report a crime, the police cannot protect you from the criminal getting his own back . . . you never get any thanks from the police for helping them . . . the police don't tell us enough about *how* we can help them . . . you can't trust people who give information to the police . . . if the police came to my door, the neighbours would wonder what I'd done wrong . . . it's the public's job to report people to the police, even for trivial offences . . . some people don't 'have a go' because there is a danger of getting badly hurt . . . some offenders get such light sentences, it's a waste of time reporting them to the police . . . some people would only report children to the police if it was very serious . . . people who go to the help of the police often end up by getting arrested themselves . . . there are some things I wouldn't report to the police because I might do the very same thing myself . . . some people would not help the police because they might get their names in the papers . . . if you've helped the police, they get to know you and never leave you alone . . . some people would like to help the police but they feel they can't do anything on their own.

The questioning procedure was as follows.

Q.1   "Generally speaking, if you had the chance, how helpful would you be to the London police?" *The respondent is allowed to talk out in order to get him thinking about the matter. After this, he is asked*: "Which of these comes nearest to how helpful you would be?" *He is shown a card presenting a 'helpfulness' scale in the form*: I WOULD BE VERY HELPFUL/ I WOULD BE QUITE HELPFUL/ I WOULD NOT BE PARTICULARLY HELPFUL/ I WOULD NOT HELP AT ALL.

Q.2   *Whatever the response chosen, the respondent is asked*: "Why is that?" *and the response is probed.*

Q.3   *Respondents who would be less than* QUITE HELPFUL *are asked*: "What do you think could be done to make you *more* willing to help the police?" *The response is probed.*

Q.4   *Respondents who were* QUITE *or* MORE WILLING *to help the police are asked*: "What do you think could be done to make people more willing to help the police?" *The response was probed.*

Q.5   "Now I'm going to read out some ways in which people can help the police. The first one is — — — —." *(One of the eleven 'ways' is read out* e.g., 'reporting something you've had stolen'). "Have you yourself ever helped the police by — — — —?" *(The 'way' is read out again.)*

Q.6   *Before going on to the next item, the respondent is asked, with regard to that same 'way'*: Suppose that in the future there was an occasion when you could help the police by — — — — *(interviewer reads out that 'way' again*). How willing would you be to do that?" *The respondent is shown a choice of answer card.*

Q.7   *After all eleven 'ways' have been dealt with through questions 5 and 6, the interviewer says*: "You remember you said you would not be willing to — — — — *(interviewer repeats this 'way')* in the future. Why would you not be willing to do that?" *The question is subject to probing. Other ways in which the respondent would not be willing to help are dealt with in the same manner.*

Q.8   *If respondent has claimed he would be less than willing* 'to appear in court as a police witness' *he is asked*: "Will you please tell me whether you agree or disagree with this statement". *The interviewer reads out the first of five statements about appearing in court, namely*: "I would not want to give evidence in court if it would help the police". *The question is then repeated for each of the other four statements, which are*: I would not want to give evidence in court because it takes up too much time . . . I would not want to give evidence in court because the lawyers might make me look foolish . . . I would not want to give evidence in court because I'd get no

88

compensation for money lost through time off work . . . I would not want to give evidence in court because I just don't like being inside a court.

Q.9 "I am going to read out some things that people have said about the police. I would like you to tell me whether you think they are TRUE or NOT TRUE. Here is the first — — — —. *(The first of seventeen statements is read out.* e.g. 'the police get fed up with people who come to them over trivial things').*" This statement itself is also presented visually, with the choice of reply between* TRUE *and* NOT TRUE *just below it. The interviewer asks:* "Do you think this is TRUE or NOT TRUE?" *The same question is now asked with regard to each of the other sixteen statements, each being shown on a strip card just above the basic response card showing* 'TRUE' *and* 'NOT TRUE'. *All seventeen statements are set out above.*

SECTION 8: Concerning factors or situations that may dispose the respondent against the London police.

In this section of the questionnaire, the respondent is asked to rate each of thirteen statements as true or false. These statements postulate points of view of a kind that, if held by the respondent, might reasonably be expected to dispose him against the police. The thirteen statements are as follows: The police have lost touch with people now the police drive around in cars . . . The newspapers are always too ready to report things that show the police in a bad light . . . It depends what mood a policeman is in whether he reports a motorist or not . . . The police don't investigate properly complaints brought against them . . . Television programmes are always too ready to show the police in a bad light . . . It's often the police on point-duty that cause the traffic jams . . . Policemen are never around when you need them . . . The police can't be bothered dealing with petty crime . . . Once a person has a criminal record, the police never leave him alone . . . The police spend too much time doing office work and not enough time on the beat . . . Some policemen go out of their way to arrest people so that they'll get promoted quicker . . . The more expensive your car, the more likely you are to get away with motoring offences . . . Police are always too ready to side with the authorities against the ordinary person.

Next, they were asked to consider a series of ten statements postulating police behaviour of an illegal or an undesirable kind (e.g., 'London police steal things at the scenes of crimes', 'London police hush up complaints made about them'). They were asked to say of these whether they thought they ever happened and, if so, how often they thought they happened and had they come across such behaviour personally. The other eight of these ten postulated forms of behaviour were as follows: London police use unfair methods to get information . . . London police plant things on people . . . London police tell lies in court . . . London police beat people up in police stations . . . London police take bribes . . . London police use too much force when arresting people . . . London police do not allow arrested persons to get in touch with their family or solicitor . . . London police force their way into people's homes without a warrant.

89

The questioning procedure itself took the following form.

Q.1   "I have here some statements about the police and the public in London. I want you to tell me for each whether you think it is TRUE or NOT TRUE. (*Pause*). Here is the first one — — — — (*The interviewer reads out the first statement*, e.g., 'The police have lost touch with people now that the police drive around in cars'). Do you think that it is TRUE or NOT TRUE?" *The other statements are dealt with in the same way. For this reactions sequence, the respondent works from a self-completion booklet, marking his replies on this (for later transfer to a coding system).*

Q.2   "Some people say that the London police do things they shouldn't do. Others disagree. I am going to read out some of these things, and I want you to tell me if you think they *ever* happen (*Pause*). Here is the first (*Read out statement*. e.g., 'London police steal things at the scenes of crimes')". *Interviewer shows visual aid presenting this statement and asks*: "Do you think this *ever* happens?"

Q.3   *If the respondent says 'Yes', he is asked*: "How often do you think this happens?" *And is offered a choice of reply from a card presenting the rating scale*: VERY OFTEN/ FAIRLY OFTEN/ NOT VERY OFTEN/ HARDLY EVER HAPPENS.

Q.4   *For each activity endorsed as ever happening, the respondent is asked*: " Have you ever come across this personally?" *If the respondent says he has not come across it personally, he is asked* "How did you come to hear about it?"

SECTION 9: Concerning views about the powers of the police.

In this section of the questionnaire, the respondent was asked to say if he thought the police had too much or too little power or about the right amount. If 'too much' or 'too little', he was asked to explain in what ways they had too much or too little power and the question was subject to probing. He was then asked to consider two statements relating to police discretion and to say if he considered them true or not true. These were: If a policeman sees someone doing something wrong, he can choose whether to ignore it or not. . . . . . The police can decide when to take people to court and when not to. Where the respondent thought the statement was true, he was asked if he thought it a good thing or a bad thing that the police should have this choice. The questioning procedure itself took the following form.

Q.1   "Some people say that the London police have too much power in some ways. Others say they don't have enough. Which one of these statements do you agree with?" *The respondent is shown a choice of answer card offering the answers*: TOO MUCH POWER IN SOME WAYS/ NOT ENOUGH POWER IN SOME WAYS/ ABOUT RIGHT. *The order of these choices is subject to rotation.*

Q.2 *If 'TOO MUCH' or 'NOT ENOUGH', the respondent is asked*: "In what ways do they have TOO MUCH/ NOT ENOUGH POWER?" *The response is probed.*

Q.3 "I am going to read out to you a couple of statements about the police. I want you to tell me, for each of them, if you think it is TRUE or NOT TRUE. The first statement is: — — — — *(interviewer reads out the first statement (see above))*. Do you think this is TRUE or NOT TRUE?" *If respondent says 'TRUE', he is asked*: "Do you think it is a good or bad thing that the police have this choice?" *The second statement is dealt with in the same way.*

SECTION 10: Concerning contact with and knowledge about some aspects of policing; some related opinions.

In this section of the questionnaire, the respondent was asked the following questions.

Q.1 "Do you know where your nearest police station is?" *If 'Yes'*: "Can you tell me where it is?"

Q.2 "Do you know the names of any policemen or policewomen who are on duty around here?" *If 'yes'*: "Can you tell me what their names are?"

Q.3 "Do you know whether any policemen or policewomen *live* near here?"

Q.4 "In what way is most of the police work done in this area?" *Respondent is offered a choice, on card, between*: 'ON FOOT'/ 'ON BICYCLES' / 'ON MOTOR CYCLES' / 'IN CARS'.

Q.5 "In what way would you *like* most of the police work to be done in this area?" *Respondent is offered the same choice as in question 4.*

Q.6 "About how often, on average, do you see a policeman or police-woman in uniform around here?" *Respondent is offered a choice, on card, between*: 'ONCE A DAY OR MORE' / 'SEVERAL TIMES A WEEK' / 'ONCE A WEEK' / 'TWO OR THREE TIMES A MONTH' / 'ONCE A MONTH OR LESS' / 'NEVER'.

Q.7 *If respondent says 'NEVER' to question 6, he is asked*: "How do you feel about never seeing a policeman or policewoman in uniform around here?" *This question is subject to probing.*

Q.8 "How often *would you like* to see a policeman or policewoman in uniform round here?" *Respondent is offered a choice on card, between*: 'MORE OFTEN'/ 'LESS OFTEN' / 'SATISFIED WITH THE WAY IT IS'.

Q.9 Have you ever looked at a leaflet dealing with *crime prevention?*" *If 'yes'*: "Where did you see it?"

91

Q.10 "Now I want to ask you a few questions about different *types* of police. First of all, traffic police. How would you recognise a traffic policeman if you saw one?" *The question is subject to probing.*

Q.11 "In fact all traffic police use either white cars or white motorbikes. (*Pause*). I would like you to tell me how you feel about these traffic police." *The question is subject to probing.*

Q.12 "Have you ever heard of police called the Special Constabulary or 'The Specials'?"

Q.13 *If 'yes' to Q.12 the respondent is asked:* "As far as you know, does The London Police Force have any 'Specials' in it?" *If 'yes' ask:* "In what ways are 'the Specials' in London different from ordinary policemen in London?" *If 'no' to the first part of Q. 13, the respondent is asked:* "In what ways are 'the Specials' different from ordinary policemen?" *The question is probed.*

Q.14 "As you probably know, in London, Traffic Wardens are doing some of the traffic duties that police used to do. *(Pause)* Do you think this is a good thing or a bad thing?"

Q.15 *Whatever the reply to Q.14, the respondent is asked:* "Why do you say that?" *The question is probed.*

Q.16 "Generally speaking, how well do you think Traffic Wardens do their job? You can choose your answer from this card." *Respondent is offered a card choice between:* 'VERY WELL' / 'FAIRLY WELL'/ 'NOT VERY WELL' / 'BADLY'.

SECTION 11: Background and classification details.

In this section of the questionnaire, the respondent was asked numerous questions about himself and his background. This information was to be used principally for classification purposes.

The full details of these questions are presented in the Appendix to the full report of the Adult study* and what follows is limited to a listing of what the 36 background and classification questions were about, namely: respondent's age at time of interview and at time of ceasing full-time education; educational or other qualifications obtained or being sought; marital status; whether respondent is a head of household; most recent job of respondent/ head of respondent's household; whether respondent has ever been on the civilian staff of any police force; whether anyone in the respondent's household has the use of a motor vehicle and various details about such vehicle(s); whether the respondent himself drives a vehicle, the extent of his driving, whether his company or firm

* "Relations between the Metropolitan Police Force and the London public. Part I: a study of the attitudes, beliefs and behaviour of adults in London in relation to the Metropolitan Police Force" Survey Research Centre (1972).

provides him with a vehicle, whether the respondent regularly drives a vehicle to work or in the course of his work; whether the non-driver has *ever* been a driver and if so when last; whether the non-driver ever travels as a passenger with a motorist and if so to what extent; the extent of the respondent's use of television and whether respondent watches certain programmes including some that feature the police; similarly with respect to radio listening; the daily and Sunday newspapers regularly read by the respondent, whether he reads any *local* newspapers; frequency of respondent's attendance at the cinema; household composition with respect to number and age; whether respondent is a British citizen, the country in which he was born and (where relevant) duration of residence in Great Britain; whether respondent has ever taken part in picketing, in a demonstration or in a protest march; respondent's involvement in any motoring or parking offence or associated court action; whether the respondent has, for reasons other than motoring offences, ever been stopped, questioned, searched, arrested by the police, appeared in court on a charge, been fined or sentenced for an offence; whether respondent has ever served on a jury in a police case; whether the respondent knows any police officer personally and the frequency with which the respondent sees the officer best known to him; has respondent or any member of respondent's family ever made a complaint against the police; the respondent's political alignment. In addition, a rating was made of the respondent's social class, and a record entered of respondent's sex, type of dwelling and floor number and whether the respondent is living on an estate.

Appendix II
A condensed form of the Police Questionnaire

INTRODUCTION AND PREPARATORY QUESTIONING

The interviewer briefly introduced himself and the enquiry and secured the respondent's permission to use a tape recorder.

SECTION 1: Concerning the police respondent's opinion about how the public feels towards the police.

In this section of the questionnaire, the police respondents used rating scales to indicate *what they thought the public felt about the London police.* These ratings were in terms of the degree to which the public was regarded as *satisfied* with the police, as *trusting* the police, as *respecting* the police, as *being at ease* with the police, as *liking* the police. These ratings were to allow comparisons to be made of the public's actual view of the police and what the police *thought* were the public's view of them. In addition, police respondents were asked to say what proportion of the public they considered: take the police for granted . . . don't want to be friends with a police officer off duty . . . don't want to be friends with a police officer on duty . . . think the police are always out to get them . . . think the police are bent.

The questioning procedure took the following form.

Q.1 "As I said, one of the things we want to find out is how *you* think the public feels about the Metropolitan police. In your opinion, how does the public feel about the Metropolitan Police?" *This question is not probed. It is asked solely to bring forward in the respondent's mind his normally available thoughts about this matter.*

Q.2 "Now I'm going to show you some cards. For each one, I want you to choose the statement which is closest to the way you think *the general public* feels about the Met. Police." *The respondent is shown a card listing the following possible answers*: THE PUBLIC DOESN'T FEEL AT ALL SATISFIED WITH THE POLICE/ THE PUBLIC DOESN'T FEEL VERY SATISFIED WITH THE POLICE/ THE PUBLIC FEELS FAIRLY SATISFIED WITH THE POLICE/ THE PUBLIC FEELS VERY SATISFIED WITH THE POLICE. *His choice is coded on the questionnaire. The order of these possible answers is reversed for one half of the sample. The respondent is now told*: "The rest are done in just the same way" *and he is taken*

94

through four more rating operations, dealing respectively with:
RESPECT FOR THE POLICE/ LIKING FOR THE POLICE/
TRUST OF THE POLICE/ FEELING AT EASE WITH THE
POLICE.

Q.3   "I am now going to read out some statements about how the public
       may or may not feel towards the Met Police. I want you to tell me,
       for each one, what proportion of the public you think feel this way.
       (*Pause*) The first one is: − − − − (*Interviewer reads out the first
       statement*, e.g., 'The public takes the police for granted.'). What
       proportion of the public − − − − (*Interviewer reads out the first
       statement again*)?" *The respondent is shown a card offering a range
       of possible answers, namely*: NOBODY OR HARDLY ANYBODY/
       ABOUT A QUARTER OF THE PUBLIC/ ABOUT HALF THE
       PUBLIC/ ABOUT THREE QUARTERS OF THE PUBLIC/
       EVERYBODY OR ALMOST EVERYBODY. *The chosen response
       is coded.*

       *This procedure was repeated for the other four statements as listed
       above.*

SECTION 2: Concerning the powers of the police.

In this section of the questionnaire the respondent was asked to
consider certain powers or practices of the police and to say with
respect to each whether the police should have more or less power.
These powers or practices were referred to as: stop and search . . .
powers and procedures when making an arrest . . . solve civil
disputes . . . deal with juveniles who break the law . . . deal with
drunken drivers . . . have access to any place of public assembly,
like cinemas and parks . . . enforce the payment of fines . . .
enforce obscenity laws . . . deal with children who break the law . . .
allow demonstrations . . . search suspects' homes. With respect to
each of these, the respondent chose a reply from the following:
THE POLICE ON THE GROUND SHOULD HAVE LESS POWER/
THE POLICE ON THE GROUND SHOULD HAVE MORE POWER/
THE POWER OF THE POLICE ON THE GROUND IS ABOUT
RIGHT. Where respondents said the police should have more or less
power, they were asked what changes they wanted, and to say what
effects such changes might have on relations between police and
public.

The questioning procedure was as follows.

Q.1   "I'm going to ask you about certain powers the Met. Police may
       exert and practices they may employ. (*Pause*) I'm going to read out
       a list of statements, each concerning a power or practice of the
       police. I want you to tell me, for each one, whether you think the
       police on the ground should have more power, less power, or
       whether the power they have is about right. The first is − − − −
       (*interviewer reads out first item, e.g. 'stop and search'*). Do you
       think the police on the ground should have more power or less
       power or do you think the power they have to − − − − is about
       right? *Interviewer shows answer card and the respondent chooses*

a reply. This procedure is repeated for each of the other items. After this, Questions 2 and 3 are asked with respect to each item for which 'More' or 'Less' power is desired.

Q.2 "You'll remember that you said the police on the ground should have more/less power to — — — — (*interviewer reads out this power or practice*). What changes would you like to see in the power they have?" *The question is subject to probing.*

Q.3 *"What effect would the kinds of changes you suggest have on relations between the police and the public? Please choose from these:"* *Respondent is shown a choice of reply card displaying:* VERY GOOD EFFECT/ SLIGHTLY GOOD EFFECT/ NO EFFECT/ SLIGHTLY BAD EFFECT/ VERY BAD EFFECT.

SECTION 3: Concerning the characteristics that the police respondents think the public attributes to the police.

In this section of the questionnaire, the police respondents were asked to say how they felt the public rated the police in terms of various characteristics, namely: friendly, rude, courteous, frightening, kind, interfering, fair, calm, bullying, efficient, dishonest, intelligent, distant, secretive, well-trained. The questioning procedure used was as follows.

Q.1 "Now, I am going to read out some words which the public might or might not use to describe the Met. Police (*Pause*). Let's take the first: — — — — (*interviewer reads out the first characteristic, e.g., 'friendly'*). In your opinion, does the public think the police are, in general, — — — — (*interviewer reads out the characteristic again*).
    The response to this open-ended question, which is purely for 'warming-up' purposes, is not coded. Whatever the reply given, the interviewer next asks: "How — — — — (*the characteristic is repeated*) does the public think the police are in general?" *The respondent is asked to choose his reply from a card presenting a scale in the form:* EXTREMELY/ VERY/ FAIRLY/ JUST A BIT/ NOT AT ALL.
    This rating task is repeated for each characteristic against the same scale, the latter being kept continuously in front of the respondent. Responses are progressively coded.

SECTION 4: Concerning the views of the police respondent about how helpful the public is towards the police.

In this section of the questionnaire, the police respondent was first asked to say how helpful or otherwise he regarded the public as being. After this, the police respondent was asked to say, of each of different kinds or groupings of people how helpful he had found them to be. These groupings were as follows: children under 14, juveniles (aged 14-16), young people (aged 17-24), old people (aged over 65), students, Indians and Pakistanis, demonstrators, shop-keepers, vagrants, skinheads and greasers, lorry drivers, West Indians, long-haired Hippy types, delivery men, Irish people, taxi-drivers, Africans, prostitutes, middle class people, working class people, upper class people, stall-holders, private motorists. From those rated as 'fairly' or 'very' helpful, the police respondent was asked to choose choose the three he regarded as most helpful, ranking them in order a 1, 2, 3. He was asked to give his view as to why the top rated group was helpful. The police respondent was next asked to name the least helpful three and say why he thought the bottom rated group was unhelpful. After this, he considered different 'ways' in which the public might help and rated public helpfulness in terms of them. The 'ways' considered were as follows: reporting something they've had stolen . . . answering questions for the police during an enquiry . . . helping at the scene of an accident . . . reporting a disturbance in a house in their neighbourhood . . . helping a policeman when he's in a dangerous situation . . . telling children to look on police as their friends . . . reporting someone they believe is about to commit a crime . . . appearing in court as a witness in a police case . . . telling police when they think someone is selling stolen goods . . . reporting someone they believe to be in possession of drugs . . . reporting a motorist for driving dangerously . . . reporting vandalism to the police.

The questioning procedure was as follows.

Q.1   "Which of these comes closest to how helpful you think the general public is?" *The respondent chooses his reply from a rating scale presented to him on a card:* VERY HELPFUL/ FAIRLY HELPFUL/ NOT PARTICULARLY HELPFUL/ NOT AT ALL HELPFUL.

Q.2   "Now I have here a form listing kinds of people. Please read it through." *After respondent reads it, the form is taken back and the interviewer says:* I want you to tell me which kinds of people are VERY HELPFUL to you or FAIRLY HELPFUL to you in the course of your work, and which kinds of people are NOT PARTICULARLY HELPFUL, or NOT AT ALL HELPFUL to you in the course of your work. If for any of them you cannot decide, simply say so. Here is the card." *Respondent is passed a choice of answer card which groups* 'VERY HELPFUL' *and* 'FAIRLY HELPFUL' *under* 'HELPFUL' *and* 'NOT PARTICULARLY HELPFUL' *and* 'NOT AT ALL HELPFUL' *under* 'NOT HELPFUL'. *The interviewer says:* "Here is the first: — — — — *(the interviewer reads out the first group,* e.g.,'children under 14'*). Are these people helpful or not helpful? Choose your answer from the card." *The rest of the listed groups are dealt with in the same way, the choice of answer card remaining in front of the respondent throughout. The interviewer ticks the groups rated helpful and puts a cross against those rated unhelpful.*

Q.3   "Please look at the kinds of people you have said are helpful to you. They are the ones I have ticked. (*The interviewer passes the form back to the respondent*). From these, please choose the three kinds of people that you think are most helpful. Put a '1' in the box beside the group you think MOST HELPFUL, a '2' beside the NEXT MOST HELPFUL, and a '3' beside the NEXT MOST HELP-FUL." *(After this, the interviewer takes back the form and asks question 4).*

Q.4   "Let's take the people you have ranked '1' — — — — (*interviewer reads out name of group*). For what reason are they helpful?" *The question is subject to probing.*

Q.5   "Now, please look at the kinds of people you have said are not helpful to you in the course of your work. They are the ones I have put a cross against. Please rank three of these kind of people, putting a '1' beside the group you think LEAST HELPFUL, a '2' against the NEXT LEAST HELPFUL, and a '3' against the NEXT LEAST HELPFUL."

Q.6   "Let's take the people you have ranked '1' — — — — (*interviewer reads out name of this group*). For what reasons are they not helpful?" *The question is subject to probing.*

Q.7   "I have here a list of possible ways in which the public might help the police. For each of them, I want you to tell me how helpful you think the general public is. (*Pause*) Here is the first — — — — (*interviewer reads out first way of helping*, e.g., 'reporting something you've had stolen') How helpful is the general public in this way? Choose your answer from the card." *The respondent is asked to choose his reply from the array listed in question 1 above. The other statements listed above were dealt with in the same way.*

SECTION 5: Concerning groups that the police respondent thinks cause trouble for the police.

In this section of the questionnaire, the police respondent is asked to say which of a list of groups of persons create problems for the police and which do not. This list included the following: tourists, homosexuals, children (aged under 14), juveniles (aged 14-16), young people (aged 17-24), old people (aged over 65), stall-holders, skinheads and greasers, lorry drivers, political extremists, shop-keepers, prostitutes, West Indians, vagrants, judges and magistrates, football fans, working class people, middle class people, upper class people, Africans, long-haired Hippie types, Irish people, taxi-drivers, drug addicts, lawyers, demonstrators, private motorists, Indians and Pakistanis, students, delivery men. Amongst those rated as causing problems for the police, the topmost three were identified. For each of the three, questions were asked to find out: if the police respondent thought that ALL members of this group created problems or only some of them; if only 'some of them', what were the characteristics of these 'some'. Of the topmost of the three, the police respondent was questioned to find out WHAT problems this group caused for the police, WHY in his opinion it caused problems and what he thought should be done to IMPROVE relations between this group and the police.

The questioning procedure was as follows.

Q.1   "I have here a list of people, some of whom may create problems or a lot of work for the Met. Police. I want you to read through them." *The list is given to the respondent and then taken back.* "Please tell me which kinds of people you think create problems or a lot of work for the police, and which DO NOT create problems for the police. If for any one of them you cannot decide, simply say so." *The interviewer reads out from the list and the respondent indicates 'yes' or 'no'. These replies are marked as tick or cross on the list.*

Q.2　"Now, please look at the kinds of people you have said create problems or a lot of work for the police. I'd like you now to rank three of these kinds of people, putting a '1' in the box beside the group you think creates most problems or work, and so on.

Q.3　*The interviewer identifies the group marked '1' and asks in relation to it:* "Let's take the people you have ranked – – – – *(Refer to rank 1 and name it)*. Would you say ALL kinds of – – – – or SOME kinds of – – – – create problems or a lot of work for the police?" *The interviewer codes 'some' or 'all' and then deals similarly with groups ranked 2 and 3.*

Q.4　*For the group ranked '1' proceed as follows if the answer to question 3 was 'some'.* "I'm going to hand you some cards and on each one you'll find a number of characteristics." *The respondent is passed four cards respectively presenting the following arrays for respondent selection:* male, female, male and female . . . upper class, middle class, working class, all classes . . . Indians and Pakistanis, West Indians, English/Scottish/Welsh, Irish, immigrants who are not coloured or Irish, all nationalities . . . children, young people, middle-aged people, elderly people, all ages. *The interviewer then says:* "Now I want you to choose from the characteristics on these four cards, those which most closely describe the kind of – – – – *(interviewer reads out name of this group)* who create problems or a lot of work for the police. Look at each card in turn, and choose just one characteristic from each card." *The chosen replies are coded.*

Q.5　*The same procedure is applied for each of the other top three if it has already been rated as 'some' through question 3.*

Q.6　"What problems do – – – – *(interviewer reads out group ranked as '1')* cause for the police?" *The question is subject to probing.*

Q.7　"Why, in your opinion, do – – – – *(the group ranked '1' is named again)* cause problems for the police?" *The question is probed.*

Q.8　"What do you think should be done to improve relations between – – – – *(the group is named again)* and the police?" *The question is probed for* WHAT, BY WHOM *and* BY WHAT MEANS

SECTION 6: Concerning the social philosophy of the police respondent.

In this section of the questionnaire, the police respondent is asked for his opinions about the public and for his views about the way society is or should be. More specifically, he was brought to consider the following matters.

99

1) The way members of the public relate to each other with respect to the following terms: kind, suspicious, honest, selfish, reliable, apathetic, friendly, violent.

2) The various views put to the police respondent about the way society is or should be were as follows: The ideal society is one where everybody has his place and accepts it . . . No one should be punished for breaking a law that he thinks is immoral . . . People make friends only because friends are likely to be useful to them . . . If it weren't for youthful rebellion, there would be less progress in the world . . . Society is constantly threatened by a minority dedicated to its overthrow . . . Only when people have got what they want in life should they concern themselves with the injustices of the world . . . The ordinary citizen really can have an influence on Government decisions.

3) Also in this section of the questionnaire the respondent was asked to rate as true or false certain statements bearing on 'people and the law'. These were: Children nowadays have no respect for authority . . . Drug addicts have got where they are through their own fault . . . Demonstrators are not committed to the causes for which they demonstrate . . . Coloured people are less intelligent than white . . . Criminals get off with sentences that are too light . . . Meths drinkers have got where they are through their own fault . . . Users of soft drugs should be dealt with just as severely as users of hard drugs . . . Practising homosexuals should be severely punished . . . People with long hair and hippy clothes are over-permissive and immoral . . . immigrants should be obliged to adopt the British way of life . . . Irish immigrants are trouble makers . . . People who sexually assault children deserve corporal punishment . . . Women are inferior to men . . . Motorists think that they own the road.

4) There were in addition five more statements for the police respondent to judge, these bearing on the officers own approach to law enforcement: Once a police officer has made a decision, he should stick to it regardless . . . It is more important for a police officer to be physically strong than to have an understanding of other people . . . Practical experience is more valuable than any academic qualification . . . It is more important for a police officer to show his authority than to try to understand a person's problems . . . Physical strength is more important than intellectual ability.

The questioning procedure used in this Section was as follows.

Q.1 "In this next section, I am interested *only* in *your own opinions* about the London public in general. I am going to read out a list of words that could describe the behaviour of members of the public *towards each other*. For each of the words, tell me how *you* think the public behave towards each other. *(Pause)* Let's take first: — — — — *(the interviewer reads out the first characteristic, e.g. kind).* Do you think that members of the London public in general are — — — — towards each other?" *The response is not coded. The interviewer then asks:* "How — — — — would you say the public are towards each other? Choose your answer from this card." *The respondent is offered a card with the choices:* EXTREMELY/ VERY/ FAIRLY/ JUST A BIT/ NOT AT ALL. *This procedure is continued for the rest of the listed ways of behaving, with the choice of response card in front of the respondent throughout.*

100

Q.2　"You have told me that the public are − − − − (*rating is given*) suspicious towards each other. Do you think this is a good thing or a bad thing?"

Q.3　"I am going to read out some statements and I want you to tell me, for each one, whether you think it is *true* or *not true*. You may choose your answer from this card." *The respondent is presented with a card showing 'TRUE' and 'NOT TRUE' and the statement to be judged, e.g., 'The ideal society is one where everybody has his place and accepts it,' is presented on a strip card just above that choice of reply. The rest of the statements are dealt with in the same way.*

Q.4　"Now, this time the statements are about various *sections* of the public. Again, I want you to tell me whether you think they are *true* or *not true*. Look at this same card." *The same card system is used as in question 3, this time with a new set of statements dropping down on to it just above the choice of answers* (e.g., 'Children nowadays have no respect for authority').

Q.5　"Now I am going to read you a few statements which could apply to the police. This time I want you to tell me whether you *agree* or *disagree* for each of them. Here is the card." *The respondent is shown an AGREE/DISAGREE card with the first of the statements* (e.g., 'Once a police officer has made a decision he should stick b' it regardless') *on a strip card just above it. The interviewer then says: "* − − − − *(the first statement is read out).* Do you agree or disagree?" *The response is coded and the other statements are dealt with in the same way.*

SECTION 7: Concerning the police respondent's attitude towards aspects of his work that have a bearing on police/public relations.

In this section of the questionnaire, the police respondent was asked about various aspects of his working conditions, of working methods and of police practices where these might reasonably be thought to bear on relations between police and public. In all cases, the questioning system involved the respondent in agreeing or disagreeing with statements to the effect that certain things occur or should be done. Wherever the respondent agreed with a statement (in the form of a proposed change or a postulated situation) he was asked what effect he thought this would have on relations between police and public.

1)　The statement relating to *working conditions* were as follows: Wherever possible, police officers on duty should wear plain clothes when they visit people's homes . . . Wherever possible, police officers should live in the community rather than in Section Houses or groups of police houses . . . Police officers should have more opportunity to take part in community activities in their on-duty hours . . . The police view should be presented more forcefully in an attempt to change laws that they think are unfair or unenforceable

101

. . . Complaints against police officers should be investigated by suitably qualified people outside the Force.

(2) The statements relating to working *methods* were as follows: More uniformed officers should be walking their beats instead of driving around in cars . . . More police officers should be Home Beat officers . . . Traffic Wardens should take over more of the traffic duties that the police now do . . . The Specials should take over more of the duties the regular police now do . . . It should be official practice to give women officers more opportunity to carry out a wider range of police work . . . Every police officer doing specialized duties should be encouraged to do a period of general duties from time to time.

(3) The statements relating to police practices were as follows: Often one of the deciding factors as to whether a police officer books a motorist or not is the officer's mood . . . In order to catch criminals police are justified in providing opportunities for crime to happen . . . Once a person has a criminal record, the police never leave him alone . . . The police tend to be too secretive about some aspects of their work . . . The police are the first to want to see a bent copper brought to justice . . . Police officers are too ready to cover up for colleagues they know have done something wrong.

The questioning prcedure used was as follows.

Q.1 "Now I would like to ask you about certain aspects of the work of the Met. police which may affect police relations with the public. First I am going to read out some statements about working *conditions*. Please say whether you *agree* or *disagree*. Choose your answer from this card." *The interviewer presents a choice of answer card showing 'AGREE' and 'DISAGREE'. He reads out the first statement about working conditions* 'Wherever possible, police officers on duty should wear plain clothes when they visit people's homes' *and asks*: "Do you *agree* or *disagree*?"

Q.2 *If respondent agrees with the statement, he is asked*: "What effect do you think this would have on police relations with the public? Look at this card." *The respondent is shown a card presenting the following possible replies*: A VERY GOOD EFFECT/ A SLIGHTLY GOOD EFFECT/ A SLIGHTLY BAD EFFECT/ A VERY BAD EFFECT/ NO EFFECT.
Question 1 was asked of each statement and question 2 whenever the respondent agreed with the statement offered in question 1.
Similar questions were asked with respect to each of the other two groups of statements.

SECTION 8: Concerning the respondent's position about factors that affect public relations.

In this section of the questionnaire, the police respondent was asked for his views: about how to improve relations between police and public, about the effectiveness of various police activities designed to improve public relations; about the ways in which the mass media present the police and the possible effect of this on police-public relations; about which organisations could do most for police-public relations and what they should do, and which do most *harm* to police-public relations.

The various police activities referred to were: crime prevention exhibitions . . . crime prevention leaflets . . . leaflets on making a complaint against a police officer . . . special projects to deal with specific problems organised by Community Liaison officers . . . recruitment publicity campaigns . . . 'Police Five' . . . Leaflets on rights when arrested . . . talks and visits to schools and playgrounds . . . advisory clinics for specific groups organised by Community Liaison officers . . . The Juvenile Bureau Scheme . . . open days at police stations.

The different ways in which the mass media present the police were listed as: 'newspapers — they are always too ready to present the police in a bad light' . . . similarly television and radio . . . 'newspapers — when criticising the police, they don't give the *police* enough opportunity to tell their side of the story' . . . similarly for television and radio . . . 'when criticised by the media, the *police* don't take enough opportunity to tell *their* side of the story' . . . most television programmes dealing with police show them as kind and understanding' . . . 'newspapers always publicise police acts of bravery' . . . 'most radio programmes on the police show them as intelligent thinking people'.

The organisations judged by the police as most and least helpful were as follows: parent-teacher associations; trade unions; local councils; education authorities; the courts; local community relations committees; immigrant associations; organisations dealing with citizen's rights; (e.g. National Council for Civil Liberties); national union of students; local residents' associations; social work agencies; probation service; youth clubs and youth organisations; the Church; Parliament; the Home Office.

The questioning procedure used was as follows.

Q.1   "What do you think the Met. Police should do to improve their relations with the public? By this I mean both activities that they *now* do and new activities that they could do *in the future. "The question is probed.*

Q.2   "Now I'd like to ask you about some community relations, public relations and publicity activities of the Met. police. For each of these activities I'd like you to tell me what effect you think it has on police relations with the public. The first is — — — — (*The first activity is read out* e.g., 'crime prevention exhibitions'). What effect do you think — — — — has/have on police relations with the public? Please choose your answer from this card." *This card offers the respondent a choice between*: VERY GOOD EFFECT/ SLIGHTLY

103

GOOD EFFECT/ NO EFFECT/ SLIGHTLY BAD EFFECT/ VERY
BAD EFFECT. *Each of the eleven items listed above is dealt with in
this way.*

Q.3 "I have here some statements about how the police are presented by
newspapers, television and radio. For each statement I want you to
tell me if it is *true* or *not true"*. *The ten statements listed above are
presented in turn against a background card showing* 'TRUE' and
'NOT TRUE'.

Q.4 *For each statement endorsed as 'TRUE', the respondent is asked*:
"What effect does this have on police relations with the public?
Choose your answer from this card." *The choice of answers offered
is the same as that presented in question 2 above.*

Q.5 "Finally, I have here a list of different organisations. Please read it
through." *After reading the list, the respondent is asked:* "Please
tick the three organisations that you think could do most to
improve relations between the police and the public."

Q.6 *For each organisation ticked, the interviewer asks*: "What should it/
they do to improve relations between the police and the public?"

Q.7 "Now please put a cross by the three organisations that you think
have done most harm to relations between the police and the public.
These organisations may be the same as or different from the ones
you've chosen in the previous question."

SECTION 9: Concerning background and classification details.

In this section of the questionnaire, the respondent was asked
numerous questions about himself and his background. This
information was to be used principally for classification purposes.
    Full details of the questionnaire are presented in the Appendix
to the full report of the police study* and what follows is limited to
a listing of what the 59 background and classification questions
were about, namely: age at time of interview; height, weight;
citizenship, place of birth, how long living in the United Kingdom;
age of finishing full time education excluding police training college,
types of school attended, examination qualifications; father's
occupation; last three jobs held by the respondent before joining the
Metropolitan Police Force and length of time in each; whether
respondent has ever been in any other police force or on the
civilian staff of any police force; whether he has ever served in the
Armed Forces and if so whether this was as National Service or as a
regular serviceman; whether he has ever been a cadet in any of the

---

*   Relations between the Metropolitan Police Force and the London
public, Part III: a study of the attitudes, beliefs and behaviour of
police officers in the Metropolitan Police Force in relation to the
London public." Survey Research Centre (1973)

Armed Forces, a member of a school Combined Cadet Force or a School Officer's Training Corps; year of joining the Metropolitan Police Force; whether he is thinking of leaving the Force before due date of retirement from the Force and if so why; his main duties in the Force at present and length of time doing these; main duties immediately before that and duration of these; nature of vehicle(s) driven or ridden when *on-duty* and miles per week on each class of vehicle; nature of vehicle(s) driven or ridden *off-duty* and miles per week on each class of vehicle; whether involved in any community work in off-duty time and if so the nature of that community involvement and whether it takes place with people on 'his ground'; the extent to which he watches television and listens to radio; the daily, evening and Sunday newspapers that he looks at regularly; whether he looks at any local newspapers and if so which; whether he lives in a police community and if so which kind; marital status; whether living at home with his family and if so the composition of his household; proportion of friends who are police officers; present rank in the Force.